Look at THAT COIN!

BEGINNER'S GUIDE TO ALL THINGS COIN COLLECTING

MARIO CONWAY

Copyright © 2024 by J & M Associates

All rights reserved. No part of this work may be reproduced in any form or by any electronic or mechanical means, including information storage and retrieval systems, without permission in writing from the author or publisher.

Printed in the United States of America

Trademarks, Etc.

This book mentions many places, companies, product names, entities, and works that are trademarks, registered trademarks, or service marks of their various creators and owners. They are used solely for editorial purposes and are not intended in any way to infringe on the rights of the respective rights holders. Neither the author nor the publisher makes any commercial claim to their use.

Disclaimer Notice

This book is unofficial and unauthorized and has not been reviewed or endorsed by any company or authorized publisher. The opinions expressed in this book are solely those of the authors and do not reflect the opinions or policies of any association.

All content are as true and accurate as possible at the time of the writing and derived from multiple authoritative sources. The author makes no guarantees of content provided and encourages reader to complete due diligence in checking facts for themselves. This book is written to give the reader informational and enjoyable content only. No warranties of any kind are declared or implied, nor is the author engaging in any legal, financial, or professional advice. Under no circumstances is the author responsible for any misinformation, losses incurred, or inaccuracies contained within this document. All photos © J & M Associates, except photos provided to media or in general public or common public usage.

Special Acknowledgements

To Mom for supporting my hobby
To my local bank tellers for providing coin rolls for hunting
To Ben Dixon, my go-to coin dealer at my local coin show
To Seth Chandler for his support and the opportunity
to go to CA and to see his coin shop
To fellow numismatists who are as passionate
about the hobby as I am!

TABLE OF CONTENTS

It All Started with a Penny 9

Chapter 1 – Introduction to Numismatics 15
    What is Numismatics? 16
    Why Collect Coins? 16
    Benefits of Coin Collecting 17

Chapter 2 – What is Money 19
    History of Money 20
    Exploring Monetary Standards 21
    The Silver Standard 21
    The Gold Standard 22
    Fiat Currency 22
    Modern Money 22
    History of US Coin Currency 23

Chapter 3 – Understanding Coin Production 29
    Early Coin Production 30
    Modern Coin Production 32
    The Steps of Current Coin Production 32
    Die Making Process 34
    Sculpting Process 35

Chapter 4 – The Look of a Coin 37
    Parts of A Coin and Key Terms 38
    Mint Marks 40

    Coin Finishes 42

Chapter 5 – Understanding Coins **45**
    Types of Coins and Denominations 46
    Value Beyond Face: Exploring Factors that Determine Coin Worth 48
    Exploring Coins of the World 54

Chapter 6 – Reasons to Collect Coins **57**
    Historical Significance 58
    Educational Importance 59
    Artistic Value 60
    Sentimental Interest 60
    Intrinsically Rewarding 61
    Cost-Effective Hobby 61
    Investments 62
    Leaving a Legacy 63

Chapter 7 – How to Begin Coin Collecting **65**
    Getting Started 66
    Coin Roll Hunting 67
    What to Look For 68

Chapter 8 – Where to Go to Find Coins **71**
    Local Coin Shops 72
    Coin Shows 72
    Clubs and Groups 73
    Online Platforms 74
    Flea Markets and Antique Shows 74

Chapter 9 – Building Your Coin Collection **75**
    Collection Themes 76

 Collector Types 78
 Things to Consider 81
 Resources to Help You 82

Chapter 10 – Caring for Your Collection 85
 Coin Collector's Toolbox 86
 Coin Handling Advice 88
 Storing Your Collection 89
 Documentation and Safety 92

Chapter 11 – Understanding Coin Grading Scales 95
 Coin Grading 96
 Official ANA Grading Standards 96
 Coins Grading Scales and Descriptions Chart 97
 Gaps in the Scale 101
 Grading Companies 101

Chapter 12 – Error Coins 105
 Coin Error Classification System 107
 Planchet Errors 108
 Hub and Die Errors 109
 Strike Errors 111

Chapter 13 – Coins and Inflation: A Closer Look 115
 Understanding Inflation 116
 Coping with Inflation: Coin Collecting Strategies 118

Chapter 14 – Navigating Misnomers in the Coin Market 121
 Identifying Coins and Misconceptions 122
 Types of Coins with Commonly Mistaken Values 123
 Coins That Appear Valuable but Aren't 125

    Spotting Counterfeits. 128

Chapter 15 – Buying and Selling Coins **131**
    Where to Buy and Sell Coins. 132

Chapter 16 – Ethics in Numismatics **137**
    Ethical Standards 138

Final Thoughts **141**

Coin Terminology/Glossary **143**

IT ALL STARTED WITH A PENNY

It all began when I was 9 years old with a chance encounter with an odd-looking penny nestled among other coins in my Mom's spare change purse. I was looking at her change, probably counting it, when I came across this cent. It looked different than the other pennies I had seen before. I examined its distinct appearance with the greenish-brown coppery hue, the worn yet resilient features, and the iconic wheat stalks flanking its sides. I was immediately intrigued. I found out that this was the wheat penny! Little did I know at the time that this modest penny would serve as the catalyst for my entry into the captivating realm of numismatics.

Eager to explore further, I ventured to the local bank, where, as a reserved youngster, I boldly asked a teller for some pennies in exchange for my hard-earned $20 cash. To my delight, I discovered more wheat pennies in the bunch. This sparked a newfound curiosity within me and so I dug into some more research, learning about the rich history and diversity of old pennies like Indian head pennies from 1859 to 1909, but the most common ones found are dated in the late 1890s until 1907.

My journey took an exciting turn when I stepped into a nearby coin shop. From the exterior, there was nothing appealing to enter the old cement block square structure that had been painted white in the day but had aged to a dirty beige. It

had the lettering of the shop's name of Westside Coins painted on the building with highlights of orange. The single door entrance was garnished with a bell that rang when you opened it and the only welcome sign was "smile. you're on camera."

The coin shop was old, a little dingy and very unkept. Although not entirely an inviting place to spend an afternoon, here is where I was introduced to the allure of buffalo head nickels and mercury silver dimes. Along three sides of the perimeter of the store stood floor cabinet displays where you'd have to ask to see the coins that were homed within the locked glass enclosures. Sometimes I did ask to see something in the displays. In order to do so, the clutter from on top of them would have to be scooted out of the way to make room to place the coin tray on top. These were always a treat to look through but usually way above my price point. Behind those floor displays along the walls were shelves that were messy and unorganized. Papers were stacked on them that looked as if they hadn't been touched in ages. There were piles of dusty old books and some collectible figurines seemingly just placed haphazardly with the hopes of someone getting to them some day.

Standing behind the display counter with the cash register on top was a gray-haired man, the owner of the store. He always seemed preoccupied with the daily newspaper or reading from some other informative source. His thick, black-rimmed glasses would sit on the edge of his nose, but he'd occasionally glance up and ask if I was looking for anything in particular. I never knew the man's name although I visited quite regularly. Perhaps his people skills (and organizational skills for that matter) weren't the greatest, but he always was kind enough to answer any question that I had. Every once in a while, you'd hear the ring of the bell as someone entered through the door with their small container of coins. They'd try to bargain with the owner to sell for a higher price than what he was willing to give. Some walked away unable to negotiate to an agreement while others took their less than hoped for amount of cash for the trade. And,

then there were other customers who came in strictly to buy bullion because they'd heard that the cost of silver was going to skyrocket. It was interesting for me just to watch people and their reactions when buying and selling coins.

But it didn't matter to me how personable the owner was or how the room looked; I just was there to play seek-and-find with coins. You see, there were those boxes and bins sitting on tables in the middle of the small square gray-hazed room. These storage containers were filled with old coins and a variety of U.S. and foreign coins. Some were loose and I could just dig in the box amongst the coins and grab a hold of one that caught my eye. I'd feel its texture and get a real good look at the details. Others were in cardboard coin holders with prices randomly marked on the slip with blue or black ink. Also written on some of those cardboard flips were the names of the coins for their identification. I would just pull up the little stool there, sit a spell, and rumble through these little treasure boxes for quite a while. I think I could've stayed for hours, maybe days! But, my parents' patience would soon wear thin, so I'd pick out a coin or two to purchase and then we'd be off until another day. I'd visit that coin shop at every chance I could when I could persuade my parents to stop. Unfortunately, only my memories remain of that coin shop as it was torn down and no longer exists today.

What I can't recall is exactly how I found out about the existence of coin shows. I just know that on one cool fall day, I got to go to a weekend coin show in town. This was way different from the coin shop that I had been frequenting. In a way, it was overwhelming to me at first. Nevertheless, attending this coin show opened my eyes to a plethora of coins I had never known existed. I stepped into a convention room that was lined with table after table of so many collections of coins. The room was bright and filled with mostly older men roaming about the tables vying for the next opportunity to buy or sell a precious coin. Moving in and out amidst these gentlemen, I would overhear their conversations and

noticed that they were friendly and liked to talk about the weather, politics, day to day life and of course, coins!

It was during this event that I experienced an act of generosity from a coin dealer when I was observing coins at his tables. I had inquired about an old silver coin whose date and most details were weathered away. However, I could distinguish that it was from Mexico. This was something that the adults, the

coin dealer himself and those standing around him, could not do. This dealer was amazed that I could figure that out and gifted me the coin which surprised me and ignited a deep appreciation for the kindness and camaraderie within the numismatic community.

Walking around the coin show, I was fascinated to see the many displays as each dealer had their own kind of collections. Some were into bullion, others into junk silver, and others into rare coins. I fondly recall walking around and seeing a 1930s old bust dime and thought, "Neat! I'm going to buy that!" Well, I got that coin and then bought a Morgan silver dollar too! I felt very happy with my new acquisitions and time spent at the coin show. I felt that the dealers genuinely enjoyed talking to me mostly because they thought it was rare that at my age, I not only had a deep interest but that I had so much knowledge about coins. They were impressed and were calling me "a walking encyclopedia" of coins. I was hooked! By the time I left, I had a few newly acquired coins and definitely knew I'd be coming back to coin shows!

As my collection grew, so did my passion for coins. I read all the material I could get my hands on about coins. I had gotten the "red book" and read it from cover to cover able to recite it mostly from memory. Birthdays and holidays became opportunities to acquire new treasures,

each coin holding its own story and significance. One very special occasion was my 10th birthday, which was my "golden" birthday, my Mom gave me my first gold coin which was a 1/10-ounce gold dime.

As the years passed in my youth, I might have been a little different from other kids with my coin hobby as I preferred spending time at banks in lieu of sporting or social events. Bank tellers knew me by name, as I was their most regular customer seeking out half dollars. In fact, I remember the joy I received upon discovering my first rare 1967 40% silver half-dollar. Shortly afterwards, I had the continued happy surprise when I found a coveted Benjamin Franklin half dollar from a box I had received from the bank. I am always proud to show the tellers what I had discovered the next time I returned to the bank. Even the tellers and security guards today are quick to ask me what I have found recently. To those who question, I pull out my newest find from my pocket and disperse all my knowledge about the coin.

Recently I was blessed by being chosen to attend a rare and exclusive opportunity held by Witter Coin University that provided numismatic training. This was an amazing experience from my first flight all the way to San Francisco, California to being trained by the best and well-known names in the industry! I learned fundamental values of numismatics, coin grading, and ethics. I got to hear the stories and teachings of many famous numismatists. This experience enabled me to meet some of the nicest people I have ever met who shared the love for coins just like me. I will be forever grateful for the support I received there from the founder, Mr. Seth Chandler, and from the other instructors. This was

an opportunity that I could not have afforded nor even imagined, so this was a dream come true. I am proud to call myself a numismatist!

Presently, I spend my days eagerly scouring banks for rare, error, and silver coins, continuously expanding my knowledge and collection. I attend the coin shows and talk to the dealers, sit a while and look at their coins. Further, I was encouraged to broaden my horizons by creating outreach methods like using social media as a teaching tool. I do this as I think it is important to give back to others in this way. This is one reason I am writing this book.

Looking ahead, I am excited about the future that lies in front of me. I want to continue to learn more. I envision myself continuing to buy, sell, and trade coins, all while sharing my passion with others who, like me, have been captivated by the allure of numismatics. Thank you for allowing me to share a bit about how I stumbled upon this fascinating interest and for me, how it more than "just a hobby" as it has become an integral part of my life. It is my true pleasure and purpose to help others learn of the value and intrigue of coins and the endless possibilities and hidden treasures that await us in the world of coin collecting.

Sincerely,
Mario Conway

CHAPTER ONE
INTRODUCTION TO NUMISMATICS

Welcome to the intriguing world of coin collecting! Numismatics is a big word that is seldom heard outside the "coin world." While it may be hard to pronounce at first, it simply means the study and collection of coins and money. It's a intriguing hobby enjoyed by people of all ages and all backgrounds, offering endless opportunities for deep exploration, expanding one's learning, and for the simple enjoyment of it.

What is Numismatics?

You may be wondering, *what exactly is numismatics?* The official definition of numismatics is the study and collection of coins and currency. It involves examining coins from different countries, time periods, and designs to learn about their history, artistry, and cultural significance. To put it in a different way, imagine if you came across an old box of coins from different countries that you'd never seen before. Then, you started examining and looking up each coin's design as if you are uncovering a mystery. That's what numismatics is all about – exploring these coins to learn about the people, places, events, and time periods that they represent.

Numismatists, or coin collectors, often research the stories behind the coins they collect, whether it is uncovering accounts of empires and rulers, or learning about everyday life throughout history. But besides the stories, coin collectors can also have an attraction to different key dates or precious metals or even obtaining various collections. There may be individual preferences, but the glue that binds all numismatists together is that they enjoy collecting and learning all about coins and currency which becomes a favored pastime of many.

Why Collect Coins?

People collect coins for lots of reasons just as the individual preferences vary. One common reason is because numismatists really enjoy history and want to

learn more about different cultures from around the world. Who doesn't love a good story, right? Well, many of the coins have a story to tell, whether it's about ancient civilizations, famous leaders, or important events. Thus, collecting coins lets you hold a piece of history right in your hands and learn about the world in a tangible way. Beyond the history and stories, there are many more reasons why people will collect coins. We will get into more reasons why people collect coins later.

Benefits of Coin Collecting

Every person has had experience and some knowledge with coins, even in a general way like making everyday business transactions. Having coins is a necessary part of life as it is money; in fact, my mother taught me necessary money and math skills at a very young age by using real coins to handle and even allowed me to pay change at the stores. However, actually collecting coins goes much deeper than that. It offers numerous benefits beyond just acquiring valuable pieces. First, it's not only a hobby that is enjoyable, but it is educational too. It promotes curiosity, critical thinking, and research skills as you investigate the history and significance of each coin. Additionally, coin collecting can be a rewarding investment, with certain coins appreciating in value over time. Another benefit is that it is an interest that can be enjoyed by yourself, with your family members, or socially with others, as collectors often gather at coin shows, clubs, and events to share their passion and knowledge. And, it really doesn't matter if you are just starting out or you've been collecting for years because coin collecting offers benefits to all ages for endless opportunities for discovery, education, and enjoyment.

These aforementioned are just a few of the reasons and benefits of coin collecting, but we will cover more in depth later in this book. Moreover, we will get into some of the details on how to begin in a simple way. I think the main key is just having a curiosity and a desire to learn. Beyond that, it's important to also

 have some goals and a plan of action for this exciting hobby to help you jump into the numismatic world.

CHAPTER TWO

WHAT IS MONEY

History of Money

Before we get into the focus of this book which is the world of U.S. coins, it's important to understand the history of money itself. Learning about the origins and evolution of money gives us valuable insights into how societies developed and functioned over time. By understanding this historical context of money, we can better appreciate the significance of coins and their role in shaping economies, cultures, and civilizations. Money has been around for thousands of years, and its history is as fascinating as the coins themselves. While a deeper look into this topic may be of interest, that is for another book. Instead, here is a simplistic and brief history lesson on the progression of money from its earliest forms to the coins we use today.

Bartering

Since creation before people used coins, they used a system called bartering to trade goods like food, clothing, and tools or to exchange services. This meant swapping one item for another without using money. For example, a farmer might trade a basket of wheat for a new pair of shoes from a shoemaker or for a piece of cloth from a weaver. This system worked but had limitations as it was not always easy to find someone who had what you needed and wanted what you had. Further, as societies grew larger and more complex, they also needed a more convenient way to trade.

The Invention of Coinage

Around 2,500 years ago, in places like ancient Greece and Asia Minor (modern-day Turkey), people began using metal coins as a form of money.

These coins were made from precious metals like gold, silver, and bronze and were stamped with symbols or images to show their value. Trading became much easier because everyone agreed on the value of the coins. Really, this standard

form of currency revolutionized trade, making transactions more efficient and accessible.

The Spread of Coinage

As trade routes expanded and empires grew, the use of coins gained popularity and spread to other parts of the world. In ancient Rome, coins called denarii were the currency of choice and used to pay soldiers and buy goods. Similarly, during China's Han Dynasty, round coins with square holes in the center were widely used for transactions.

Exploring Monetary Standards: Silver and Gold

In the history of money, silver and gold have played significant roles as monetary standards. These precious metals were used to back the value of currency and coins, providing a stable foundation for economic transactions.

The Silver Standard

The silver standard was a monetary system in which the value of currency was directly linked to a specific weight of silver. One notable example is the Spanish dollar, also known as the piece of eight, which became widely used as a trade coin in the 16th century. This coin contained 90% silver and served as the basis for many currency systems around the world. A silver Morgan Dollar minted in the United States during the 19th century, containing 90% silver, represents an era of the silver standard in American currency.

The Gold Standard

Similarly, the gold standard was a monetary system where the value of currency was backed by a fixed amount of gold. One of the most famous implementations of the gold standard was the British Gold Sovereign, introduced in 1817. This coin contained 7.32 grams of gold and became the benchmark for currency valuation in many countries during the 19th and early 20th centuries.

Fiat Currency

While coins were the primary form of money for many centuries, paper money began to emerge during the Middle Ages. In China, merchants used paper receipts as a form of payment. While in Europe, banks issued paper notes that could be exchanged for coins. Eventually, paper money became more common, especially as printing technology improved. This significant advancement offered greater convenience and flexibility in transactions.

In the 20th century, most countries transitioned from metallic standards to fiat currency systems, where the value of money is not backed by physical commodities but by the trust and confidence in the issuing government. This shift marked a significant departure from traditional monetary systems based on silver and gold.

Modern Money

Today, most countries utilize a combination of paper money and coins as their currency. These coins and banknotes are issued and regulated by governments and central banks. They primarily are backed by the country's economy. While digital forms of payment, like credit cards and online banking, are very popular, coins continue to play an essential role in everyday transactions and

as collectible items for numismatists around the world. Understanding the evolution of monetary standards provides valuable context for coin collectors and enriches the appreciation of numismatic treasures from different periods of history.

History of US Coins for Currency

Now that we've briefly explored the history of money from ancient times to the present day, let's narrow our focus to the coins used in the United States. While coins from around the world have their own stories and significance, this book will primarily focus on the rich variety of coins minted in the United States.

The United States has a long and diverse history of coinage, spanning from colonial times to the modern era. U.S. coins come in different denominations, designs, and compositions, each with its own unique features and historical background. From the iconic Lincoln cent to the majestic American Eagle silver dollar, U.S. coins offer a wealth of opportunities for collectors to explore and appreciate.

Throughout this book, we will look into various aspects of U.S. coin collecting, including how to start your collection, how to identify coins, and tips for caring for your coins. However, I feel it is important to first acknowledge the history of U.S. coins since it is so essential to this hobby.

Circulating Coins

Before the U.S. had its own mint in 1792, there were many different kinds of coins used in the country. These coins came from both inside and outside the nation and were used in trade, business, and everyday life.

During the Colonial Period, people used a mix of coins from places like Britain, Germany, and Spain. Among these, the Spanish milled dollar was especially

popular because it had a lot of silver and kept the same value over time. Since smaller coins were hard to find, people sometimes cut these silver dollars into halves, quarters, and smaller increments to use for smaller purchases.

After the Revolutionary War, things changed. Each state could make its own coins and decide their value. This made things confusing because the same coin could be worth different amounts in different states.

In 1787, Congress started debating making national coins. They approved making copper cents called "Fugio," meaning "I fly" in Latin. These coins were made of 0.36 oz of copper and had a picture of a sundial representing fleeting time on the obverse. A chain of 13 links was on  the reverse representing unity between the states. Also known as the "Franklin cent" and by some accounts, this coin was designed by Benjamin Franklin. But when the Constitution was ratified in 1788, the discussion about national coins started again, leading to more changes in American money.

The Coinage Act of 1792

The Coinage Act of 1792 was a big moment for American money. It made the first official mint in Philadelphia and set up a system for making coins. This system used decimal numbers, like we do today, and included coins worth 100 parts.

The Act made the U.S. dollar equal to the Spanish milled dollar, a coin people already knew well. It also set up smaller coins like the half, quarter, eighth, and sixteenth, making things easy for people who were used to these coins. Different metals were used for different coins. Copper made the half cent and cent, which were important for everyday transactions. Silver made coins like the

half dime, dime, quarter, half dollar, and dollar. Gold coins like the quarter eagle, half eagle, and eagle ($10) showed the country's hopes for a strong economy.

Interestingly, in 1792, while building the Mint, 1,500 silver half dimes were made secretly in a nearby cellar. They may have been gifts for dignitaries but shows a hidden part of early American money history.

On March 1, 1793, the Mint made 11,178 copper cents for circulation. However, these new coins caused some issues with public opinion. They were considered bulky for small change and people were unsatisfied with the design of Liberty's seemingly frightened expression and the chain of 15 links on the back. In response, the Mint quickly changed the design to appease the people.

Even though the Coinage Act stopped states from making their own coins, it let foreign coins still be used until the Mint could make enough coins for everyone. With this Act, Congress made American money more reliable, setting the stage for a stronger money system.

Challenges to Circulation
Incorporating U.S. coins into everyday use faced many challenges. Although the Mint worked hard to produce the coins, there were still problems. One main issue was making enough copper cents for circulation. Further, copper became expensive, so in 1857, Congress stopped making half cents and made cents smaller to save copper.

Silver and gold coins were being coined in 1794 and 1795, but they didn't circulate. This was because their value didn't match with what people thought they were worth. The Coinage Act of 1792 set the silver to gold ratio at 15:1,

which differed from the world markets. Gold coins were worth less than silver, so they were sent overseas or melted down. Silver was also mostly exported or stored.

In the early 1800s, banks also created a challenge. When banks provided gold and silver to the Mint to make coins, they mostly wanted the larger denominations in return. This meant that they did not coin the smaller denominations of coins such as half dimes, dimes, and quarters which is what the public needed for their daily transactions.

To fix these problems, Congress made new laws. They stopped making some coins such as the silver dollar and gold eagle. Further, they changed the weights of coins and the ratio of gold to silver. They also opened new Mint locations and improved how coins were made to greatly improve production and circulation. Finally, in 1857, Congress banned foreign coins used as money. These changes helped U.S. coins become more valuable and common in everyday life.

U.S. Coins Design Changes Through the Years

When the United States was just getting started with The Coinage Act of 1792, rules were made about how our coins should be portrayed. These rules said that every coin should symbolize freedom. The coins were to be inscribed with the word "LIBERTY" and the year it was made on the obverse side. For gold and silver coins, an eagle had to be on the reverse side along with the words "UNITED STATES OF AMERICA." Copper coins, on the other hand, were only required to show the denomination; however, a wreath became the standard design.

At first, instead of putting real people on the coins, like George Washington or other presidents, Congress chose to personify liberty with the Liberty figure, a symbol from the American Revolution in contrast to how the monarchy

in Britain are depicted on their money. Lady Liberty was not only a symbol from the American Revolution but has origins as an ancient Greek-Roman goddess. Thus, the basis for her design of classical-style clothing and holding a pole with a cap (representing freedom) on top.

For over 150 years, Lady Liberty was on our coins. But in 1909, Abraham Lincoln took her place on the penny. After that, presidents started to appear on other coins (see chart). Lady Liberty's last appearance on a coin was in 1947 on the Walking Liberty half dollar.

Year	Domination	President
1909	Penny	Abraham Lincoln
1932	Quarter	George Washington
1938	Nickel	Thomas Jefferson
1946	Dime	Fraklin D. Roosevelt
1964	Half Dollar	Jhon F. Kennedy
1971	Dollar	Dwight D. Eisenhower

This chart illustrates the timeline of when presidents started to appear on various denominations of coins in the United States.

CHAPTER THREE

OVERVIEW OF COIN PRODUCTION

Considering that billions of circulating coins and numismatic products are made each year, it goes without saying that it is a major undertaking that the U.S. Mint and the other mints go through for production of those coins. From using state of the art technology to die making to the sculpting process, many factors contribute to making all the different coins. For well over two centuries, there has been transformative changes that make the U.S. Mint one of the largest mints in the world.

Early Coin Production

The journey of coin making began with humble beginnings when the early Mint was established in a three-story brick building in Philadelphia. It relied on manual labor, horses, and rudimentary machinery. The Coinage Act of 1792 laid the groundwork for American coinage, authorizing the Mint to produce copper, silver, and gold coins. However, in those early days, the Mint struggled with imprecise processes, producing a limited number of coins at a painstaking pace. They made the first coins – 11,178 copper cents – but it was a slow process by only making a few coins every minute!

Throughout the 19th century, advancements in technology revolutionized coin production. The advent of steam power in 1816 marked a significant turning point, as steam engines powered rollers and cutting presses, streamlining the coining process. The Mint's acquisition of steam-powered coining presses in 1835 further propelled efficiency, with each press capable of producing approximately 100 coins per minute! This monumental leap in production capacity not only accelerated the pace of coin making but also paved the way for the Mint's expansion and the establishment of branch mints across the country.

1856, Workers flattened metal strips through steam-powered rollers, Hutchings' California Magazine

The transition to steam power heralded a new era of innovation and progress in coin production. In 1838, the opening of branch mints in Charlotte, Dahlonega, and New Orleans necessitated the introduction of mint marks to distinguish coins originating from different facilities. This practice, however, was not adopted by the Philadelphia Mint until 1942 when the iconic "P" mint mark made its debut. Interestingly, the first coin to have the "P" mint mark was the 35% silver Jefferson "war nickel."

During the 20th century, the Mint went through many changes by embracing technological advancements. Not only had the third Philadelphia Mint facility opened in 1901, but over the decades, electricity replaced steam power, automation was increased, and computer-controlled machinery to further enhance efficiency and precision.

Modern Coin Production

Today, the Mint's state-of-the-art facilities employ cutting-edge technology to produce coins at unparalleled speeds. Computer-controlled machines meticulously strike each coin with remarkable accuracy, ensuring consistency and quality in every piece. With modern presses capable of producing 750 coins per minute, the Mint's production capacity has reached staggering heights, enabling it to meet the nation's growing demand for circulating coinage.

> **Fun Fact:** Did you know the Mint didn't just make coins? They also made special medals for important events. And they even made coins for other countries, like Venezuela and the Philippines. In fact, they made coins for over 40 other countries. They did all this while still making sure America had enough coins to use every day. It's amazing how much the Mint has done over the years!

The Steps of Current Coin Production

The U.S. Mint is responsible for producing the nation's circulating coins, as well as bullion and collector coins. The process of making coins involves several steps, from creating the initial design to packaging the finished product. This is a simplified description to provide an overview of the coin production process at the U.S. Mint.

John Sinnock, Chief Engraver of Roosevelt dime

Step 1: Design Approval

Once the Secretary of the Treasury approves a coin design, Mint artists transform the design into a 3-D sculpt. This sculpt is then digitized to create the coin dies. (*see the information following on the die making and sculpting processes.)

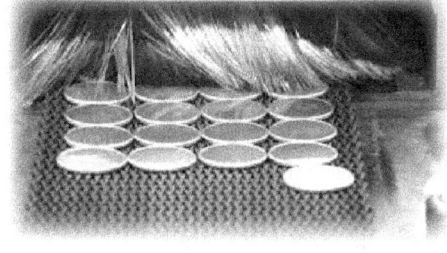

Step 2: Blanking
Blanks, which are flat metal discs that will become coins, are created for the various denominations. The Mint buys coils of metal and punches out blanks using a blanking press at a spectacular rate of 14,000 blanks per minute. These blanks are then transported to the annealing furnace.

Step 3: Annealing
Blanks are heated in an annealing furnace of up to 1,600 degrees Fahrenheit to make them softer and more malleable. This oxygen-free environment prevents tarnishing. They are then quickly cooled in a quench tank filled with a special solution to lower temperature and prevent sticking.

Step 4: Washing & Drying
The cleaned blanks are washed to restore their original color and then dried using steam.

Step 5: Upsetting
The edge of the blank is raised to create a rim, which protects the final coin from wear and tear. This process is called "upsetting" the edge. The blanks are then inspected to ensure they meet specifications. Blanks with rims are called planchets and ready for striking. Special planchets meant for proofs and uncirculated coins, go through burnishing. This process has particular cleaning agents and small metal pellets to create a smooth and polished surface. Then, an employee will hand-dry them with towels.

Step 6: Striking
Planchets are fed into coin presses where they are struck with the coin design. The press forces the obverse and reverse dies together against the planchet to create the coin. Circulating coin presses can strike up to 750 coins per minute! Coins are struck with different amounts of pressure and speeds depending on the type of finish for the coin. And, a proof is struck at least twice.

Step 7: Bagging & Packaging
Once the coins pass inspection, they are counted, weighed, and placed into bulk storage bags. Numismatic (collector) coins are packaged using robots and automated machines, while bullion coins are packaged in monster boxes for shipment.

Die Making Process

Die making at the U.S. Mint is a meticulous process that ensures every coin bears the intricate design intended for it. Here is a simple overview of the steps involved in creating these essential tools for minting US coins.

Step 1: Die Blanks
To start, steel rods are cut into sections and formed into cone-shaped blanks. These blanks serve as the foundation for the dies.

Step 2: Master Hub & Die
A CNC machine engraves the design onto a master hub, which is then used to create master dies. These dies transfer the image onto the cone-shaped die blanks with incredible force.

Step 3: Working Dies

The master dies produce working hubs, which in turn create working dies used for striking coins. This process ensures that the master dies remain preserved while working dies are used and replaced as needed.

Step 4: Final Dies

Working dies undergo heat treatment to strengthen them for the coin-striking process. They are tempered, engraved with serial numbers for tracking, and meticulously inspected before being deemed ready for use.

Step 5: Proof Dies

For coins requiring special finishes like proof or reverse proof, additional preparation is necessary. This includes polishing, frosting, and chrome plating to enhance the design and protect the die during striking.

Sculpting Process

I would be amiss if I didn't mention a bit more about the sculpting process of coins. In fact, the design of the coin itself is why so many people are attracted to coin collecting! Before there is a design, there is an artist behind the design. To put it simply, creating designs for coins at the U.S. Mint is like turning drawings into real-life sculptures. It starts with picking the best designs, which are then carefully checked and approved. Naturally, before coin production can even start, a design has to be given the green light. Then the artist begins to make it come alive. They use materials like clay and plaster, or digital tools, to shape the design into a 3D model.

The artist takes time to study the details, maybe even visiting places or looking at pictures to get everything just right. They add layers of clay to build up the

design and then smooth out the rough edges. After that, they might make a mold of the model to fine-tune the smaller parts.

Once the sculpting is done, the model gets scanned into a computer to make a digital copy. This digital version lets the artist make any final tweaks using special software. When the model looks perfect, it's used to make a metal stamp or die. This die is what's used to press the design onto the coins or medals. Like any good artist, the designer puts their initials somewhere on the coin like the notorious AW initials of the designer, Adolf Weiman, on the walking liberty and mercury dime. Then, once checked, the Mint is ready to start making real coins and medals for everyone to use and collect.

Adolf Weiman, Sculptor & Designer

AW Initials

CHAPTER FOUR

THE LOOK OF A COIN

Parts of a Coin and Key Terms

Before collecting coins, it's important to be familiar with some basic coin terms, including the anatomy of a coin and the different finishes. There is a Coin Glossary in the back of this book to help understand meanings of commonly used terms or jargon in the community of coin collectors. In addition, the parts of a coin, including the different finishes, are discussed in this section.

Have you ever played a game of heads and tails? We probably all have or at least seen the coin toss in a football game where the team leaders are asked to call "heads" or "tails." So, in reality these basic terms of heads and tails are referring to the front and back of a coin. More specifically the **Obverse** is the front side of a coin while the back side of a coin is called the **Reverse**.

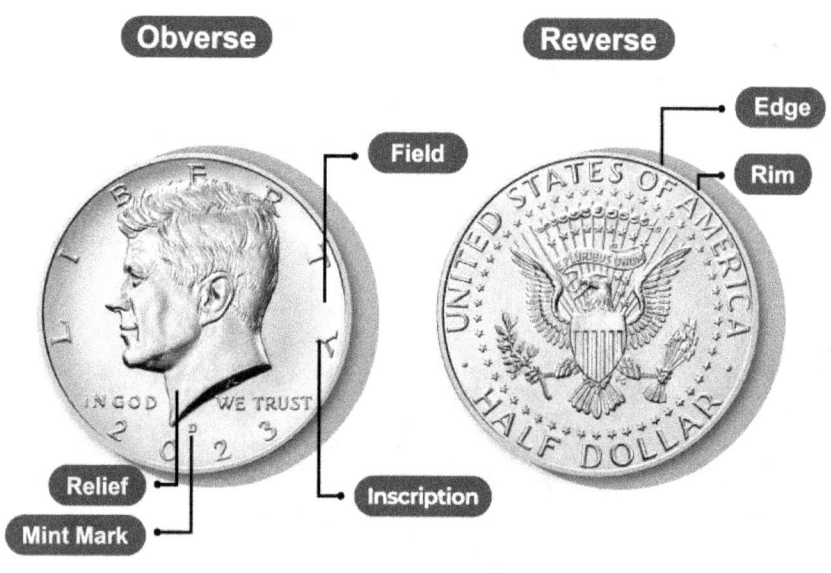

USMint.gov

Generally speaking, on the obverse ("heads") side of a coin, you can see the coin's main **Relief** or design that is raised up on the coin. This design is meant to

quickly identify what type of coin it is. For example, most people immediately recognize George Washington's bust on a coin and know the coin is a quarter. In the diagram, you'll see John F. Kennedy's face as the identifying relief on the half-dollar coin's obverse.

Comparatively, the reverse ("tails") side of the coin is of a lesser type of design or a more commonly used design. In the example of the half dollar shown, the back side of the coin shows the American eagle symbol.

You can also find the **Inscription** or main words that is inscribed on the coin. Sometimes this is also referred to as the legend. In the diagram, the common word of LIBERTY is on the coin's obverse, along with the words In God We Trust. While on the reverse, the inscription reads UNITED STATES OF AMERICA and HALF DOLLAR.

In the **Field** section of a coin, it is the flat part or the "background" if you will. It is not used for a design or inscription. Everything else on the coin is raised up from the flat surface of the field.

A feature of a coin that a beginning coin enthusiast should not ignore is the **Edge** of a coin. Surprisingly perhaps, the edge can be of great significance if you are coin roll hunting. The edge is the outer rim around the coin; where you should especially hold your more valuable coins. The edges could be varied by either a plain edge, reeded, lettered, or even decorated.

Plain Edge

Reeded Edge

Lettered Edge

Decorated Edge

USMint.gov

Mint Marks

The **Mint Mark** of a coin can have quite a significance to a coin collector. The mint mark is a small letter on a coin indicating where a coin was made. They hold the maker responsible for the quality of a coin. When the U.S. used precious metals such as gold and silver to make circulating coins, a commission evaluated the metal compositions and quality of coins from each of the Mint facilities. The evaluations ensured that each facility produced coins to the correct specifications. Current U.S. mint marks are P (Philadelphia), D (Denver), S (San Francisco), and W (West Point).

Initially, the sole operational branch of the Mint in Philadelphia obviated the necessity for mint marks. However, the establishment of additional branches prompted the adoption of mint marks through legislative action in 1835. Subsequently, when Mint branches opened in Charlotte, Dahlonega, and New Orleans in 1838, mint marks debuted on U.S. coins. Despite this, Philadelphia's coins remained unmarked.

This practice changed during World War II when the composition of five-cent coins shifted due to nickel shortages. Coins produced in Philadelphia were marked with a "P" to denote their origin and the altered metal composition. After the war, normal alloy usage resumed, and the "P" mint mark ceased. However, it resurfaced in 1979 with the introduction of the Susan B. Anthony dollar coin, appearing on all denominations except the cent.

Each Mint facility was assigned a unique mint mark. (See chart below.)

Mint Facility	Mint Mark	Year Began
Charlotte	C	1838
Dahlonega	D	1838
New Orleans	O	1838
San Francisco	S	1854
Cason City	CC	1870
Denver	D	1906
Philadelphia	P	1942
West Point	W	1984

Mint Mark Tidbits

Notably, from 1965 to 1967, circulating coins bore no mint marks, a measure taken by the Coinage Act of 1965 to discourage coin collecting amidst coinage shortages. The placement of mint marks also shifted from the reverse to the obverse of coins in 1968.

The San Francisco Mint, from 1854 to 1955 and from 1968 onwards, minted coins marked with an "S." West Point joined in 1984 with a "W." Additionally, Philadelphia introduced "P" marks on circulating pennies in 2017. West Point introduced mint marks on quarters in 2019, marking the first time this facility contributed to circulating coin production.

Concerning medals, most do not bear mint marks, except for specific numismatic silver medals partially for marketing purposes. The mark can be on the obverse or reverse side, depending on how it fits into the design.

Coin Finishes

Uncirculated

Proof

Reverse Proof

USMint.gov

When you look at coins, their appearances can vary because of the different finishes that they possess. The same coin with the same year can look entirely different because of the wear or finish it has. There are 4 main categories of coin finishes: Circulated, Uncirculated, Proof, and Enhanced.

Circulated

Firstly, circulating coins (also called business strike coins) are those commonly used in daily transactions. These coins are designed to endure regular circulation without significant wear and tear, maintaining their appearance over time.

Uncirculated

Uncirculated coins represent a step up in quality, catering to collectors and enthusiasts. While they undergo the same production process as circulating coins, meticulous attention is paid to enhance their finish, resulting in a pristine and lustrous appearance. People enjoy saving their uncirculated finds.

Proof

Proof coins are revered for their impeccable craftsmanship and striking aesthetics. They feature a mirror-like background with frosted design elements, achieved through a specialized manufacturing process which involves manually

feeding burnished coin blanks into polished die presses. Multiple strikes on the coin are made to accentuate the details.

Reverse proof coins offer a unique variation on traditional proof coin finishes. In reverse proof, the background is frosted while the design elements boast a mirror-like shine, creating a mesmerizing contrast.

Enhanced
Occasionally, the Mint introduces enhanced versions of these finishes, where additional detailing or polishing is applied to specific areas of the coin. This further elevates their visual appeal and makes them stand out in collections. An example of this would be an extra frosted field of a coin.

While coins come in a variety of finishes, each caters to different purposes and appeals to collectors with varying preferences. Whether for everyday transactions or as cherished collectibles, the diverse range of coin finishes offers something for every numismatic enthusiast to appreciate. The following table outlines at a glance the differences between the finishes.

Finish	Definition/ Trait	Year Began
Circulating	Everyday coins used in transactions.	Produced with durability in mind to withstand regular circulation without significant wear and tear.
Uncirculated	High quality coins catered to collectors.	Undergoes the same production process as circulating coins but with multiculous attention to detail for a pristine appearance.
Proof	Coins with mirror-like background and frosted design.	Manufactured using a specialized process involving multiple strikes to create a mirror-like background and frosted design elements.

	- Includes reverse proof coins with frosted background and mirror-like design.	Reverse proof coins feature a frosted background with a mirror-like design, offering a unique variation on traditional proof coins.
Enhanced	Special versions with additional detailing or polishing.	Additional detailing or polishing applied to specific areas of the coin to further enhance its visual appeal and detail.

CHAPTER FIVE

UNDERSTANDING COINS

Understanding the different denominations of coins allows collectors to appreciate the history of numismatics. Whether collecting pennies, dimes, quarters, or dollars, each denomination offers unique insights into the country and specific events during a certain period of time. Many of these coins' designs are commemorative and will diversify to represent important aspects of the history and culture.

Types of Coins and Denominations

Type of Coin	Denomination/Value	Significant Designs/Changes
Pennies	One-cent	Various reverse designs depicting national symbols, landmarks, or historical events - Lincoln cent featuring Abraham Lincoln on the obverse (introduced in 1909)
Nickels	Five-cent	Various reverse designs including the Monticello, bison, and Westward Journey series - Jefferson nickel featuring Thomas Jefferson on the obverse (introduced in 1938)
Dimes	Ten-cent	Barber dime featuring Liberty with a wreath on the obverse (introduced in 1892) - Mercury dime featuring Liberty with wings on the obverse (introduced in 1916) - Roosevelt dime featuring Franklin D. Roosevelt on the obverse (introduced in 1946)

Quarters	Twenty-five-cent	Standing Liberty quarter with Liberty holding a shield on the obverse (introduced in 1916) - Washington quarter featuring George Washington on the obverse (introduced in 1932) - State quarter program with unique designs representing each state (issued between 1999 and 2008) - 1964 silver quarters
Half Dollars	Fifty-cent	Walking Liberty half dollar with Liberty walking towards the rising sun on the obverse (introduced in 1916) - Franklin half dollar featuring Benjamin Franklin on the obverse (introduced in 1948) - Kennedy half dollar featuring John F. Kennedy on the obverse (introduced in 1964)
Dollars	One-dollar	Morgan dollar featuring Liberty on the obverse with an eagle on the reverse (introduced in 1878) - Eisenhower dollar featuring Dwight D. Eisenhower on the obverse (introduced in 1971) - Sacagawea dollar featuring Sacagawea, a Native American woman, on the obverse (introduced in 2000)

It is important to note that there have been numerous coins throughout the United States history that no longer circulate. Some, like the half-cent coin were removed due to inflation reducing their value. On the other hand, others such as the two-cent piece were removed due to a lack of demand. There was the three-cent nickel, despite the "nickel" in its name which is referring to the nickel as a chemical element in its composition. And, there was even a 20-cent piece! These denominations might sound odd to us today, but all the coinage that is now obsolete could be a book in itself and it is certainly worthy of study. When these rarities are found, they are amazing to add to a collection just for the denomination value discussion alone.

3-cent nickel

Value Beyond Face: Exploring the Factors that Determine Coin Worth

While coins may have a face value stamped on them, their true worth often extends far beyond this nominal value. Understanding the factors that contribute to a coin's value is essential for collectors seeking to build valuable collections. There are various elements that influence a coin's worth as outlined below.

Rarity

One of the primary factors influencing a coin's value is its rarity. Coins with limited mintages or those that are difficult to find in circulation tend to command higher prices among collectors. For example, a coin issued in limited quantities due to historical circumstances or production errors may be considered rare and highly sought after. One such coin is the 1909-S VDB Lincoln Cent. This cent is highly coveted by collectors due to its low mintage of just 484,000 coins. This coin features the initials "VDB" of its designer, Victor David Brenner, is also considered rare because of its historical significance as the first Lincoln Cent.

Similarly, coins that were issued in limited quantities due to production errors are prized for their rarity. An excellent example is the 1955 Double Die Lincoln Cent, which exhibits a noticeable doubling of the date and inscriptions due to a misalignment during the die preparation process. Despite being relatively common in circulated condition, examples in uncirculated grades are scarce and highly sought after by collectors.

Furthermore, coins from certain time periods or series may be considered rare due to their limited survival rates. For instance, coins from ancient civilizations such as ancient Greece or Rome are inherently rare due to the passage of time and the limited number of specimens that have survived to the present day. Likewise, coins issued during wartime or periods of economic upheaval may be scarce due to factors such as hoarding, melting for their metal content, or destruction during conflicts.

Condition

The condition of a coin plays a significant role in determining its value. The condition, also known as the grade, of a coin can be assessed by grading agencies, such as the Professional Coin Grading Service (PCGS) or the Numismatic Guaranty Corporation (NGC). They are known to meticulously evaluate coins based on various criteria, including surface quality, luster, and the presence of any imperfections.

A coin that is well-preserved in mint state (uncirculated) condition, with its original luster intact and no visible signs of wear, will generally command a higher price than a similar coin with evidence of circulation, such as slight rubbing, scratches, or contact marks. Coins with full strikes, sharp details, and attractive toning are highly sought after by collectors and often fetch premium prices at auctions or through private sales. Conversely, a heavily circulated coin with significant wear to its design elements may only retain its intrinsic metal

value and carry little to no premium for its numismatic appeal. This is not to be confused with coin errors that even with imperfections are considered rare and valuable.

Historical Significance

Coins that hold historical significance or cultural importance often carry greater value in the numismatic market. Such coins often evoke profound interest among collectors due to their connection to pivotal moments in history or their portrayal of symbolic designs of a particular era.

For example, coins minted during the American Revolutionary War or the signing of the Declaration of Independence are highly sought after by numismatists intrigued by their association with key moments in the nation's past. These coins serve as tangible artifacts that bear witness to the trials, triumphs, and transitions of bygone eras, making them prized additions to historical collections.

Likewise, coins featuring iconic designs that symbolize national identity command considerable attention from collectors. The Indian Head Penny, for instance, that was minted from 1859 to 1909 bears the image of Liberty adorned with a Native American headdress, reflecting the cultural amalgamation of America's diverse population during the 19th century. Numismatists fascinated by American history and artistry often seek out these coins for their aesthetic appeal and cultural significance, thereby contributing to their elevated market value.

Furthermore, coins associated with renowned historical figures or respected institutions may also accrue greater worth in the numismatic realm. Coins featuring the likeness of influential leaders such as Abraham Lincoln,

George Washington, or Thomas Jefferson often attract collectors drawn to the personalities and legacies of these eminent figures. Similarly, coins issued by esteemed mints or bearing commemorative designs honoring significant events, such as the Apollo 11 Moon Landing or the Civil Rights Movement, hold intrinsic historical value that resonates with collectors passionate about preserving moments of societal impact.

Demand

It goes without saying that market demand absolutely plays a role in determining a coin's value. Coins that are highly sought after by collectors or those experiencing a surge in popularity due to trends or historical events may command premium prices. Factors such as rarity, condition, and historical significance can all influence demand for a particular coin.

The 1943-D Lincoln bronze wheat penny stands out as a prime example of a coin propelled by demand despite its relatively common circulation, the 1943-D penny garnered widespread attention and escalated in value due to its unique composition during World War II. This historical context imbued the coin with a compelling narrative, driving collector interest and elevating its market demand.

Societal trends or collective sentiment will generate surges in demand with particular notable events. For example, the bicentennial quarters issued by the U.S. Mint in 1975 and 1976, generated considerable excitement among collectors seeking to commemorate the nation's 200th birthday. These quarters attracted substantial demand from enthusiasts eager to acquire mementos of this occasion, thereby contributing to their elevated market value.

Demand is also impacted by the shifting preferences for specific coins by collectors which in turn drive fluctuations in their market worth. Coins featuring popular designs, iconic motifs, or sought-after mintages may experience heightened demand from numismatists seeking to enhance their collections with  coveted pieces. For example, the introduction of innovative coin series or the discovery of rare varieties within existing collections can spark fervent interest among collectors, fueling demand and driving prices upwards.

Numismatic Trends

Numismatic trends play a significant role in shaping the value of coins, with collectors often drawn to coins that align with popular themes or exhibit characteristics favored by the collecting community. In essence, numismatic trends reflect the evolving tastes and preferences of collectors, influencing the value and desirability of coins in the market.

A more recent example of a numismatic trend is the growing interest in coins featuring wildlife motifs or natural themes. Coins adorned with images of animals, birds, or scenic landscapes appeal to collectors with an appreciation for nature and wildlife conservation. For instance, the 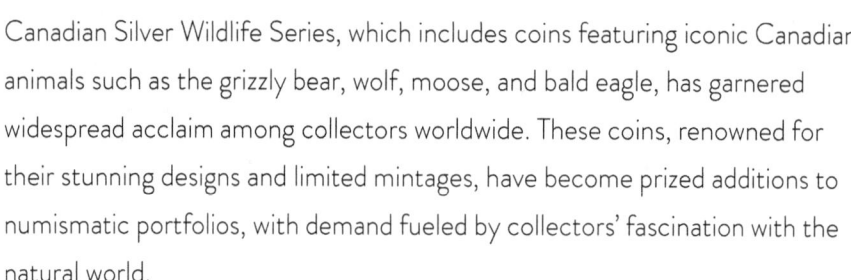 Canadian Silver Wildlife Series, which includes coins featuring iconic Canadian animals such as the grizzly bear, wolf, moose, and bald eagle, has garnered widespread acclaim among collectors worldwide. These coins, renowned for their stunning designs and limited mintages, have become prized additions to numismatic portfolios, with demand fueled by collectors' fascination with the natural world.

Additionally, coins that exhibit innovative or unconventional designs may capture the attention of collectors seeking unique and visually striking pieces.

 Coins incorporating cutting-edge minting technologies, holographic elements, or intricate patterns often generate buzz within the numismatic community, driving demand and pushing prices higher. For example, the Royal Australian Mint's Southern Sky Series, which features coins showcasing the constellations of the southern hemisphere, has captivated collectors with its innovative designs and celestial themes. As a result, these coins have become sought-after collectibles, with prices reflecting the popularity of astronomical motifs among numismatists.

Precious Metal Content

For coins made from precious metals such as gold, silver, or platinum, the intrinsic value of the metal itself contributes to its overall worth. The current market value of the metal, along with factors such as purity and weight, influences the value of these coins independent of their face value.

Consider, for example, the American Gold Eagle coin, a popular investment and collector piece prized for its gold content. Minted in various denominations, including 1/10, 1/4, 1/2, and 1 troy ounce, the American Gold Eagle commands a premium above its face value due to its composition of 91.67% gold (22 karats). The market value of gold, which fluctuates based on factors such as economic conditions and investor sentiment, directly influences the worth of these coins. During periods of economic uncertainty or currency devaluation, investors often flock to gold as a safe-haven asset, driving up demand and elevating the value of gold coins like the American Gold Eagle.

Similarly, silver coins such as the American Silver Eagle, containing one troy ounce of .999 fine silver, derive their value from the prevailing market price of silver. While their face value remains nominal, the intrinsic worth of the silver they contain fluctuates in response to market dynamics, including supply and demand, geopolitical tensions, and industrial applications. Collectors and investors alike value these coins not only for their numismatic appeal but also for their role as tangible stores of wealth in times of economic uncertainty.

Platinum coins, such as the American Platinum Eagle, offer another example of coins valued for their precious metal content. With a purity of .9995 fine platinum, these coins command significant premiums above their face value due to the rarity and desirability of platinum as an investment metal. Factors such as limited mintages, industrial demand, and geopolitical factors can influence the market value of platinum coins, reflecting the intricate interplay between precious metal prices and coin valuation. Many collectors and investors take the opportunity to acquire precious metals as assets with enduring value in an ever-changing economic landscape.

Exploring Coins of the World

Coins provide a window into the rich diversity of cultures and histories across the globe. While our focus may primarily be on U.S. coins, it's essential to appreciate the fascinating array of coins from other countries. Many numismatists add international coins to their collections for various aspects such as history, designs, denominations, and cultural significance. As discussed in Chapter 2, coins have been used as a form of currency for thousands of years, with various civilizations around the world minting their own coins. From ancient Greek drachmas to medieval European deniers and modern-day yen and euro, each coin tells a unique story about the society that produced it.

Designs and Symbols

One of the most incredible aspects of world coins is their diverse designs and symbols. These designs often reflect the cultural heritage, national identity, and historical events of the issuing country. For example, the Canadian maple leaf on the Canadian Maple Leaf coin symbolizes Canada's natural beauty and resources, while the kangaroo on Australian coins represents the country's unique wildlife. The Australian Kangaroo Gold Nugget is an iconic coin that features a depiction of a kangaroo, a symbol of Australia's unique wildlife, on its reverse side.

Denominations and Monetary Systems

Different countries have their own monetary systems, with unique denominations and values for their coins. For instance, the British pound sterling consists of coins such as the penny, shilling, and pound, each with its own value and significance. Understanding these denominations and their equivalents in different currencies is essential for collectors interested in acquiring coins from around the world.

Cultural Significance

Coins often hold significant cultural and historical importance for the countries that produce them. For example, commemorative coins issued to mark special events or anniversaries may celebrate national heroes, historical milestones, or cultural traditions. These coins serve as tangible reminders of a nation's heritage and identity. For example, the South African Krugerrand coin is made of gold and features a portrait of Paul Kruger, a former president of South Africa, on one side and a springbok, a national symbol, on the other. The Japanese Yen is Japan's currency that includes coins such as the 1 yen, 5 yen,

and 100 yen, each adorned with symbols representing the country's culture and traditions.

Exploring coins from around the world offers collectors a broader perspective on numismatics and a deeper appreciation for the global diversity of currency. From the ancient coins of Rome to the intricate designs of European currencies, the world of international coinage has something to offer for every collector.

CHAPTER SIX

REASONS TO COLLECT COINS

What are the reasons to collect coins? *Ahh, where do I begin?* First off, I think it's important to mention that the term **numismatics** is often used interchangeably with the coin collection, however it denotes more intensive study than just simply collecting coins. One way to put it is that all numismatists are coin collectors, but not all coin collectors are numismatists. Whichever way you slice it, the reasons *why* they are a collector cannot be answered so simply. Ask any coin collector as to *why* they collect coins, and the answer will probably be not one reason, but several.

I do think for anyone to collect coins, they must have a passion for it. No matter the age or where a person is from, people are drawn to this age-old pastime. Coin collecting can be traced back to ancient Greece days when it was customary to give people coins as gifts. It is a popular hobby with statistics showing that over 1/3 of the population has enjoyed this pastime at least at some point in their life.

Collections come in various types, much like the diverse reasons individuals have for them, whether it's seeking out scarce vintage coins to enhance their collection or obtaining newly issued commemorative editions. Regardless of the type of coin collection, most of the reasons why we collect what we do can be for one or several of the reasons mentioned below.

Historical Significance
As touched on in the Coins History section, coins have an intriguing history and with the plethora of coins out there, you can really dive deep into a unique and rich history of each type of coin. This alone makes coin collecting such a rewarding hobby. Every old coin has a great historical story behind it. Some

of them were created centuries ago, having a great value for the history and culture of that country.

It is also about having a real part of history in your hands; it is like having a piece from an entire story related to that coin. For example, having an old Mexican coin, like the foreign coin that I inquired about at my first coin show, can tell you a lot about the culture and history of Mexico during that time period. This could lead to research and become very educational at the same time. The same applies to any other country's coins. It is quite fascinating to think about who had that same coin in their possession long ago.

The historical history behind coins, especially old coins, is what makes collecting old coins so unique and interesting because the little coin has the power to transport you back in time. It's giving you a glimpse of the world as it was centuries ago. And this is definitely a benefit worth having!

> ***My tip:*** *Simply look up online the date and country of origin on the historical coin to get a snapshot of how it was like to live there in that time period.*

Educational Importance

Coins contain a wealth of information about the period in which they were minted and the notable figures. I think the history and educational significance go hand in hand. For instance, learning about a coin's history can create an opportunity to learn about the culture and currency of the time. The educational aspect can also include any type of learning dedicated to that coin like its origination, unique design, production, value, and any other interesting aspect or story behind it. Honestly, the educational significance is constant.

My tip: Include children or grandchildren in the educational aspect, you'll be building life-long learning and memories.

Artistic Value

It has been said more than once that beauty is in the eye of the beholder. With coins, that saying holds. Artistic value in coin collecting extends beyond mere monetary worth. While some collectors focus solely on the numismatic value of coins, others are drawn to coins for their aesthetic appeal.

For these collectors, coins serve as small canvases showcasing intricate designs, appealing imagery, and rich symbolism. Furthermore, the craftsmanship and attention to detail displayed on coins make them akin to miniature works of art that tells its own story through its artistry. These can be irresistible to those with an appreciation for art.

Coins can also connect the visual appeal to sentimental value for collectors similarly to those who adorn themselves with gold or silver jewelry. Collectors adorn their collections with the mesmerizing luster of precious metals that they find aesthetically pleasing.

Sentimental Interest

Just about everyone acquires souvenirs and mementos from important trips and adventures. On a special trip or vacationing, some people collect coins like other people collect refrigerator magnets. What better way to bring home a commemorative souvenir than a coin from the country you just visited? I don't know about you, but I think a coin will hold value over a refrigerator magnet…just saying! When I was around ten years old, I visited several countries in the Caribbean that used different coins. I traded the natives there my American coins for their coins. I

still look at those coins today with fond memories, not just of the coins, but of the experience trading with the locals there. While most of those coins hold no or little monetary value, they are precious to me. Even here in the states, when I travel occasionally, I find a local coin shop to visit and bring back a newly purchased coin as my memento. It not only adds to my collection, but I've gained a new memory to go along with it.

My tip: If you haven't before, try looking for a special coin from your next vacation spot that is representative of the area and culture.

Intrinsically Rewarding

Coin Collecting can be exciting and purposeful. In fact, many collectors, including myself, get a rush or thrill of the chase to find the "treasure." Along with that comes the satisfaction when you find a rarity or finally complete a set after months of hunting for that last elusive coin. Not only is it satisfying, there is the feeling of accomplishment. When you have set a target or goal to find a certain number of silver dimes in a month and then reach that goal, it is quite satisfying to know you have accomplished your mission.

My tip: To get the most out of your hobby, set yourself specific targets for coins you'd like to get your hands on (like 10 silver dimes a month) and start searching rolls to reach that goal!

Cost-Effective Hobby

If you've seen the price of some coins, say may smirk at this reason, but there's a saying in the numismatics world that, "Coin collecting is the only hobby that when you're broke, you'll still have money!" While that joke is tongue-in-cheek, there is definitely some truth to it. While I know that some coins can be very

expensive to purchase and some have sold for millions, anyone can start the hobby for free. It's hard to think of another hobby that requires no start up costs. Can golf, bicycling, or most other collections be free to start? Probably not! However, anyone at any age can either start for free or using their spare change. It's up to you how much you want to collect and what to collect and of course, how much you want to spend towards that collection. Coin collecting can be affordable and is why many choose to adopt and maintain this enjoyable hobby.

> **My tip:** Budgeting is important with all things, coins included. Set aside a certain amount per month to spend on finding and buying your coins- noting all costs entailed such as traveling, ordering, membership fees, etc.

Investments

Many factors determine a coin's value including grade, rarity, and popularity. Obviously, the higher the value, the more the coin would be considered as an investment. One of the great benefits of collecting coins as an investment is because of the metal content. Coins are made from different metals, such as copper, nickel, zinc, silver, gold, and platinum. These metals can be melted down and reused for other purposes. The metal content of the coins also affects the value of coins.

Certain coins are more valuable because they contain more precious metals than others. For example, a gold coin contains more worth than a copper coin. Knowing that precious metals are valuable, coin collectors may choose to have some of these types of coins to serve as a hedge against inflation or to serve as long-term investments and assets.

Generally, rare coins increase in value over the long term and can provide significant gains in many cases. Highly sought-after coins again increase the value of a coin. There are commercial organizations such as the PCGS or NGS

that offer grading services and will grade, authenticate, attribute, and encapsulate most coins. While there are no guarantees for how a coin will change in value, it usually is a safe bet to hold for the long term.

My tip: To collect coins as investments, it is important to do research from authentic and trusted sources to know about the coin in order to make smart decisions in purchasing them for your collection.

Leaving a Legacy

Some coin collections are a result of different generations gathering them. Coin collections can be a legacy to pass on to your family as a meaningful inheritance to last for multiple generations. Leaving a legacy, one that you can physically hold on, has meaning beyond the metal content of the coins.

My tip: If intending to pass on to family members, I would suggest creating a log of the coins along with writing their significant stories to go along with them. What a precious gift that would be!

CHAPTER SEVEN

HOW TO BEGIN COIN COLLECTING

Starting a coin collection is a journey that begins with some curiosity and enthusiasm. While it may seem a little daunting at first, becoming a coin collector is a rewarding and enjoyable pursuit that anyone can start. My point is that if the passion and the interest is there, becoming a coin collector is simple to do. Knowing certain basic terms associated with the hobby is key and we have gone over most of those in the previous chapters. We've also explored some of the various reasons why people are drawn to coin collecting, so now it's time to address how you can start your own coin collecting...so how does that begin?

Getting Started

Accessibility is key to starting. Chances are that you already possess the beginnings of a coin collection without even realizing it. To kickstart your collection, begin by exploring your immediate surroundings. Raid your own coin stash whether tucked away in your pocket, the car, or stored in shoeboxes or dresser drawers of your home, coins can be found in everyday places. Perhaps there's a commemorative coin you've been given as a gift or some foreign currency you've held onto from travel. If so, give it a second look, study it's design or history, and decide if you want to begin a similar collection.

Spare Change Jar

In our family, we've had a spare change jar my entire life. It is a large 64oz. glass Mason jar. To keep loose pocket change from just laying all around the house (or falling in the cracks of the couch), we  collectively throw our loose change in this jar. With everyone pitching in, before long, our loose change really adds up. We have always had a purpose for the change in that jar. We designate a specific goal for when the jar gets full to use it in some way to give back to the community or church. We basically donate it. When the jar is emptied, we come up with a new purpose. Since not everyone

in my family is a coin enthusiast as myself, I have been granted the right to go through the jar to find any coins to add to my collection but adding face value back to the jar. Perhaps, this is an idea you can incorporate into your own family. If you make a goal like we have or perhaps spend it on a nice family meal at a fancy restaurant, you'll have everyone throwing in their change.

Family and Friends

Reach out to family and friends who may have coins to spare. Offer to take their coins in to the banks for them to drop in the coin machine to get cash for them just for allowing you to look through them first. I do this with my Great Uncle. He saves all of his coins for me to look through when I come to visit. He allows me to pay him for any interesting finds. Another avenue is to reach out to those who have been gifted a collection through an inheritance and evaluate their coins for them. This may take some time to gain experience enough to be able to do this.

Coin Roll Hunting

You have a bank, right? One of the best ways to access coins is to simply ask your bank for rolls of coins. Local banks are convenient and usually will honor requests. Things to ask for specifically are customer wrapped coins and rolls of coins in whatever denomination you prefer such as pennies, nickels, dimes, quarters, and half dollars. These rolls can yield a variety of treasures, from vintage coins like wheat pennies and silver dimes to special mint proofs and commemorative editions. Take them home and start searching!

For those eager to expand their coin roll hunting further, ordering boxes of coins can provide a larger and diverse selection to sift through. Be prepared for the cost of the box or boxes when they come in which is usually once a week. You'll

quickly learn which days you need to place your order in so you can get the box the same week; otherwise, you'll have to wait until the next week's order. Another thing to note is that boxes of coins are heavy so be prepared to do some heavy lifting out to your car or use a heavy-duty rolling cart like I do for ease of transport.

> **My tip:** Know what to do with coins after you have searched them. You usually cannot return a huge amount of loose coins so instead use coin counting machines to dump the coins. It will take a while when you have large quantities to dump. Simply dispense your loose change into the coin reservoir. Then the machine counts your coins and prints a voucher with your total. Remember to check the reject pocket for any rejected coins! Then take your voucher to the bank teller to receive cash back or make a deposit.
>
> Many banks do not have these coin counting machines but there are credit unions and banks that do and may require you to be a member to use them. An alternative is to find an automated kiosk at a local retailer or grocery store to turn your coins to cash or a gift card, but there will be probably be a fee to use them.

What to Look For

When coin roll hunting, you need to have somewhat of an idea of what you are looking for in the rolls of nickels, quarters, or whatever denomination you choose. Usually collectors are looking for mainly key dates on certain coins which probably contain silver, foreign coins, proofs and of course any odd coins or errors. The following chart gives some specific examples of coins to look for according to their denomination when coin roll hunting.

Denomination	What to Look For	Key Dates	Special Notes
Pennies	Wheat Pennies, Errors	1909-1958	Look for errors like the 1983 copper penny
Nickles	Buffalos, Special Mint Proofs, War Nickles (1942-1945)	1913-1938	Look for silver nickles (1942-1945), mint mark over Monticello
Dimes	Mercury Dimes, Silver Dimes	Pre-1965	Look for silver proof dimes from 1992 to present, pre-1975 silver dimes with white edges
Quarters	W Mints, Uncirculated, 1964	1964, 2019-2020	Look for 1964 silver quarters, West Point NY with W mint mark from 2019 & 2020
Half-Dollars	Silver, Silver Kennedy Halves	Pre-1971	Look for commemoratives, mirror finish proofs, 1970 40% silver halves with only 2 million minted, 1964 silver Kennedy halves are 90% silver.

CHAPTER EIGHT

WHERE TO GO TO FIND COINS

Besides starting to look at coins in your immediate surroundings and picking up coin boxes or rolls at your local bank, you can locate coins at other locations that exist specifically for those interested in coins. These places are not hard to find, you just have to know they are there. From local coin shops to the online marketplace, you can find coins to suit your needs.

Local Coin Shops

For hands-on experience and access to a wider range of coins, consider visiting reputable local coin shops. Almost every decent sized town has one so stop in and browse- you never know what you might  find. Your local coin shop owner can help get you started with some basic knowledge of coins. When you visit friends and family out of town or go on vacation, look for the local coin shop in that town too. I find it interesting how local coin shop owners differ in their shops from décor to the coins they offer for sale.

Coin Shows

Attending local coin shows is a fantastic way to begin immersing yourself in the "coin world." This is one of my top preferred ways  to access coins. Attending shows allows you to get to know individual dealers and ask multiple questions to those who have been around the block for a while. They are usually very willing to not only show you their coins, but to teach you more about numismatics.

Regional shows are held throughout the year and offer further opportunities to connect with dealers and expand your collection. Do online searches for when the next show is in your area. In my hometown, there is a show once a month, but an even bigger coin show is about 1 hour away and held twice a year. Every single time I attend, I learn something new or am able to specifically look for certain coins to add to my collection.

There are also huge national coin shows that are held once or twice a year like the F.U.N. show which is held in Orlando, Florida. Other national shows include American Numismatic Association's National Money Show and World's Fair of Money show. Again, doing a quick online search will bring you the latest information on when and where these are held.

Clubs and Groups

Join a local coin club. Joining your local coin clubs can offer valuable insights and opportunities to learn from seasoned collectors. There are some coin clubs that meet quite regularly and it's a great way to meet fellow enthusiasts and share knowledge. Not only that, at these clubs you can swap coins or buy and sell with each other and many also have guest speakers.

The world's largest coin club is the American Numismatic Association, a non-profit organization. You may want to consider joining the ANA as it helps people discover and explore the world of money through its vast array of educational programs including its museum, library, conventions, seminars, publications and outreach programs. Further, The ANA provides a database of clubs around the world.

Online Platforms

There are some online platforms to use for your own learning similar to the ANA and then there are websites and selling platforms like eBay that can provide avenues for purchasing coins. Just exercise caution if choosing to purchase coins online. You want to be sure that the websites are trusted and from authentic sources.

Auctions, such as Heritage Auctions, showcase the rarest and most expensive coins on the market. These coins are often available only through auctions.

> *My Tip:* Compare prices to avoid overpaying and verify a reasonable return policy before ordering from any online auction, site, or platform.

Further, there are YouTube videos on coin collecting and numismatic blogs that you can help you learn more about coins. Consider joining social media groups that are dedicated to the hobby and just as passionate about it as you are. Here, you can connect with fellow enthusiasts, exchange insights, and gain valuable tips and advice in an online, much broader world.

Flea Markets and Antique Shows

I'm hesitant to include flea markets and specialty events like antique shows and so forth, but coins can be found at these various events. Coins found in these kinds of places have less competition which can encourage inflated prices. There's also the issue that has been known of the selling of "problem coins." Unfortunately, counterfeits do occur and if a deal looks too good, well then it probably is. So as always, be cautious and know your source.

CHAPTER NINE

BUILDING YOUR COIN COLLECTION

While you are building up a collection of coins, you may want to focus on a certain kind of coin. Decide what it is about coins that interest you and start from there. Are you drawn to a specific period in history and eager to acquire coins minted during that era? Or perhaps you're fascinated by special edition coins commemorating significant events and milestones. Some collectors simply like to accumulate only one thing like silver Mercury dimes. And, very commonly, there are those who are eclectic, adding a little bit of everything to their collection. There is no wrong or right way. You do you! And remember that the most important step is to simply start collecting! Your interests and collections may evolve over time, so don't hesitate to explore different themes and discover what resonates with you. But whatever your interests may be, just get started.

Collection Themes

Countries of the World

Collecting coins from different countries allows enthusiasts to delve into the rich tapestry of global cultures and histories. For example, a collector may gather coins from countries like Japan, India, Italy, and Brazil, each offering unique insights into their respective traditions, landmarks, and historical events.

Time period

Focusing on coins minted during a particular era or historical period enables collectors to immerse themselves in a specific epoch's monetary history. For instance, a collector might specialize in ancient Roman coins, medieval European coinage, or coins from the Renaissance era, providing a window into the economic and social dynamics of those times.

Coin finish

Collectors who appreciate the craftsmanship of coins often seek out different finishes to enhance their collections. Examples include proof coins with their immaculate mirror-like surfaces, uncirculated coins showcasing pristine mint luster, and bullion coins valued for their metallic composition and weight.

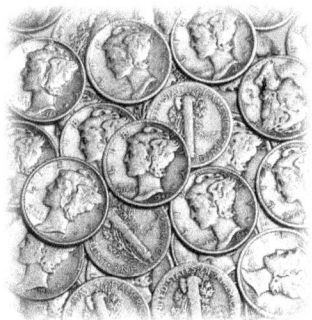

Denomination

Building collections based on specific coin denominations offers collectors a focused approach to their hobby. For instance, one might collect all denominations of a particular currency, such as pennies, nickels, dimes, quarters, and dollars, or specialize in coins of a specific value, like silver dollars or half dollars.

Mint mark

Exploring coins bearing different mint marks adds an element of intrigue to numismatic pursuits. Collectors may seek out coins from various mints, such as the Philadelphia Mint (P), Denver Mint (D), San Francisco Mint (S), and others, each contributing to the diversity of their collections.

Mint Mark "S"

Design theme

Collecting coins featuring common design themes or motifs allows enthusiasts to curate visually cohesive collections. Examples include coins adorned with

wildlife imagery, historical figures like presidents or monarchs, iconic landmarks, or national symbols such as flags, coats of arms, and emblems.

Artist

Appreciating the artistry of coin design involves collecting coins created by renowned designers whose work graces numismatic masterpieces. For instance, collectors may seek out coins crafted by artists like Augustus Saint-Gaudens, Adolph A. Weinman, or John Mercanti, whose designs have left an indelible mark on the world of coinage.

U.S. Mint sets

The U.S. Mint offers various annual sets tailored to collectors' preferences, providing convenient opportunities to acquire coins based on specific themes or series. Examples include uncirculated sets featuring coins from each mint facility,

proof sets showcasing pristine specimens, and quarter sets commemorating landmarks or events across the United States. Collectors may opt to acquire these sets to enhance their collections or as keepsakes of significant milestones in numismatic history.

Collector Types

Besides collection themes, some people are also specific in what types of coins they buy like only purchasing bullion or others will only get coins with 90% silver. I know some that prefer to purchase only coins encased in graded slabs. I sometimes prefer just to sit down at one of my local coin show's dealers and go through his bags of junk silver. In essence, there are all different types of collectors. We generalize these collectors by calling them a specific "type" of coin collector. These terms are not meant to "pigeon-hole" anyone and

of course, any individual collector may consider himself in several different categories.

Generalists

Generalist collectors enjoy building collections that span various historical periods, regions, and themes. They are fascinated by the diversity of coins and may collect examples from ancient civilizations, medieval Europe, colonial America, and modern times. For instance, a generalist collector might have a Roman denarius, a Spanish doubloon, an English shilling, and a modern American dollar coin in their collection, appreciating the unique characteristics of each.

Specialists

Specialist collectors focus their collections on specific areas of interest like any of the themes mentioned earlier. They may concentrate on coins from particular countries, time periods, or with distinct features such as mint marks or designs. For example, a specialist might collect only British coins from the Tudor period, Japanese feudal coins, or Australian coins featuring native wildlife.

Completists

Completist collectors are driven by the goal of acquiring every type of coin within a specific category. They aim to build comprehensive collections that include every variation and subtype of coin, often seeking out rare and elusive pieces to complete their sets. A completist collector, for instance, is one who endeavors to collect every date and mint mark of a particular coin series, such as all Lincoln cents or all Morgan silver dollars. One notable

example is Louis E. Eliasberg, who famously compiled a complete set of known United States coins, including rare and elusive pieces.

Foreign Coin Collectors

Collectors of foreign coins are intrigued by the currencies of countries outside their own. They enjoy exploring the rich diversity of designs, denominations, and historical contexts represented in foreign currency. A foreign coin collector might collect coins from different regions of the world, such as European euro coins, Asian yen coins, African rand coins, and South American peso coins.

Coin Hoarders

Coin hoarders prioritize accumulating coins based on their potential long-term value, often without much consideration for aesthetic appeal. They're a bit like investors because they hope the coins will be worth more in the future. They may focus on acquiring coins with high intrinsic metal content, such as gold or silver coins, as a means of preserving wealth. Examples of coins favored by hoarders include pre-1965 US silver coins, gold bullion coins like the American Gold Eagle, and ancient silver drachms.

Speculators

Speculative collectors engage in coin collecting with the intention of profiting from fluctuations in coin demand and value. They may strategically buy and sell coins based on market trends, aiming to capitalize on price changes over time. For instance, a speculator might purchase limited-edition coins from government mints and sell them at a premium when demand increases or invest in coins made from precious metals like gold and silver as a hedge against inflation.

Inheritors

Inheritors acquire coins unexpectedly as part of an inheritance, often without prior interest or knowledge in numismatics. They may inherit collections passed

down through generations, discovering valuable or historically significant coins among their newfound possessions. Examples of coins inherited by collectors include rare coins handed down from grandparents, commemorative coins from deceased relatives, and ancient coins discovered in estate sales.

Things to Consider

When considering adding a coin to your collection, it's important to ask yourself a few key questions, ensuring that each addition enhances the overall quality and value of your numismatic pursuits. The following points will help you evaluate a coin... simply just put in a little bit of time and thought to consider whether a coin is deemed valuable to you and if it is worth adding to your collection.

Appeal
Does the coin appeal to you personally? Whether it's the design, historical significance, or overall aesthetic, choose coins that resonate with you and reflect your collecting interests.

Luster
Assess the luster of the coin – how shiny and reflective is it? Keep in mind that the luster of a coin cannot be restored, so look for coins with natural shine and brilliance.

Condition

Check for any signs of damage. Scratches, bag marks, staple marks, and corrosion can significantly diminish a coin's value and overall appearance. Opt for coins that are free from major blemishes and imperfections.

Wear

Examine the level of wear on the coin's surface. Wear, often measured by grading standards, is a key factor in determining a coin's condition and value. Coins with minimal wear typically command higher prices and are more desirable to collectors.

Buying and Trading

Consider your options for acquiring coins. Are you purchasing from a reputable dealer, participating in coin shows or auctions, or trading with other collectors? Evaluate the potential risks and benefits of each method and choose the approach that best suits your preferences and budget.

Resources to Help You

Resources are sources of good information to help you, guide you, and teach you to enable a better understanding of any particular topic. In school, you might seek out a tutor in math so you can learn the math skills better or when learning how to cook a dish, you ask a good chef. We do this because we don't want to fail math or create a meal that is not edible. Instead, we want to succeed and understand better. The same with collecting coins. It is intelligent practice to seek out resources that will help us be successful in our endeavors.

Books

I hope you find this book encouraging and helpful, and I also suggest buying a guidebook too. It's essential to educate yourself about the hobby as you start collecting coins.

Learning from others is great, but you probably want additional material to have on hand. I mentioned earlier that I read the red book from cover to cover. That book was called The Official Red Book: A Guide Book of United States Coins. Investing in a guidebook like The Official Red Book, which catalogs all coins ever minted, can serve as a valuable reference tool. You need to have an idea on how coins are valued, how many were minted, etc. The Official Red Book as well as some others are updated yearly.

If you decide to collect a specific series or focus on coins from another country, there is likely a reference book out there that can give you the details for which you are looking. If you cannot find what you are looking for in reference books, the majority of information you may need for your collecting can likely be found online.

Magazines/Periodicals

Besides publications from organizations such as the ANA, I find it helpful to pick up timely periodicals. There are dozens of special magazines dedicated to coin collectors like the Coin World magazine. Many dealers will recycle their monthly magazines and place them on the tables at the monthly coin shows that are free for the taking! So definitely look for those and pick them up when you can. It makes for some good reading in your spare time.

Online Apps/Resources

Digital resources to find values of coins online are a quick and convenient tool as well. There are even apps you can download. Ask around and see what the experts are using and what they think is user friendly. I can't tell you how many times when at a coin show, I see people pulling out their phones to their go to apps to look up coin values – it helps them decide whether or not the coin for purchase is a good deal. One of the most common resources for dealers is Greysheet, which publishes current coin market values and pricing guide.

Mentor

If you can find a mentor who is willing to help show you the ropes, then consider yourself blessed. There are a few out there who WANT to teach others along the way. They feel the numismatic community is worthwhile and are enthusiastic about the hobby. So look around, ask, and see if you can find a mentor out there who has the time and the willingness to share.

CHAPTER TEN

CARING FOR YOUR COLLECTION

It's exciting to start finding coins, collecting them, and entering into the world of numismatics. Your coin collection becomes important to you, essentially being a segment of who you are as a person. To retain the value and look of your coin collection, proper care and storing are essential. Providing the proper care of your coins takes some basic supplies. Think of a carpenter on the job. Chances are that he is not just taking one tool like a hammer with him. To do his job properly, he may have quite a few tools in his toolbox, perhaps along with a hammer, he also has a screwdriver, wrench, saw, and so forth. As a coin collector, you should probably need a few items in your "toolbox" too.

The Coin Collector's Toolbox

Magnifying Glass

A high-quality magnifying glass is an essential tool for inspecting coins closely. It helps collectors examine details such as mint marks, inscriptions, and surface  imperfections. For example, a 10x magnification hand lens is commonly used by numismatists to spot minor details that the naked eye just cannot do. Research and find a good magnifying glass or loupe to help you identify features that may affect a coin's grade or authenticity. Choosing the right one for you greatly depends on the coins you plan to collect and what you plan to do with them.

> **My Tip:** This tip actually comes from my coin mentor, Mr. Chandler. I recall him saying that no matter if you have perfect vision to get a pair of reading glasses. I followed that advice and use them every time I coin roll hunt now!

Soft Cloth

When handling coins, it's crucial to use a soft cloth or pad to protect them from scratches and damage. This cloth provides a gentle surface for placing coins during examination, preventing them from coming

into direct contact with hard surfaces. A microfiber cloth or velvet padded tray is ideal for this purpose, ensuring coins remain still when you put them down.

Plastic Ruler

A plastic ruler is preferred over metal rulers because it reduces the risk of scratching coins during measurement. Collectors often use rulers to gauge a coin's diameter and thickness, aiding in the identification and classification of different coin types. For instance, a transparent plastic ruler with millimeter markings allows for precise measurements without causing harm to coins.

Coin Reference Book

As stated earlier, a comprehensive coin reference book is an invaluable resource for collectors, providing essential information on dates, mint marks, major varieties, grading guidelines, and current market prices. Examples include publications like the "Red Book" for U.S. coins or the "Standard Catalog of World Coins" for international coinage. These books offer detailed insights into the history, production, and value of various coins, aiding collectors in making informed decisions and expanding their knowledge base.

Good Lighting

Adequate lighting is crucial for examining coins accurately and identifying subtle details. Natural daylight or a bright LED lamp provides optimal illumination for viewing your coins, revealing surface characteristics, toning variations, and other important features. Proper lighting conditions ensure that collectors can assess coins accurately and appreciate their aesthetic qualities. It is recommended that you use an incandescent bulb with around 75 watts and to avoid fluorescent bulbs. I have an adjustable lamp that I keep on my desk designated for my coins and turn it on every time I coin roll hunt.

Soft Cotton Gloves

When handling your precious coins, it's advisable to wear soft cotton gloves to prevent oils, dirt, and fingerprints from transferring onto the coin

surfaces. These gloves help maintain the coins' condition and minimize the risk of tarnishing or corrosion. Collectors often opt for white cotton gloves with a snug fit to ensure dexterity while handling coins delicately. It's a good idea to remember to always hold your coin by the sides even when wearing gloves. If soft gloves are unavailable, a soft towel will also do the trick.

When simply searching through a mass amount of coins that you may have acquired (like by getting some coin boxes from the bank), use different gloves for going through these. I use disposable gloves to rummage through them as some are old and dirty and it keeps my hands clean as well.

Coin Holders or Albums

Coin holders or albums really are ideal for storing and organizing your collection safely. These protective enclosures provide a secure environment for coins, shielding them from dust, moisture, and physical damage. Examples include cardboard 2x2 holders, plastic flips, coin capsules, and coin albums with designated slots for different coin types and series. By using coin holders or albums, collectors can preserve their coins' condition and showcase their collection systematically. (*see Storing Your Collection in this section for more specific information)

Coin Handling Advice

Handling coins properly is crucial for preserving their condition and value. Start by ensuring your hands are clean before touching coins to prevent transferring oils, dirt, or moisture onto them. Hold a coin by its edges between your thumb and forefinger. When picking up a coin, always hold it by the edges to avoid

touching the faces, which can leave fingerprints or scratches that diminish their value. But again, it is a really good practice in using soft gloves when you are handling them, especially higher valued coins.

Even when handling, storing, or moving coins in different locations, always keep coins cool and dry and away from moisture which can cause discoloration. Avoid talking directly over coins; tiny droplets of saliva can also create spots on a coin. Just like fingerprints, these marks are difficult to remove.

Although this seems like common sense, be cautious not to drop coins. When coins are dropped, especially onto hard surfaces, they can be dented or scratched. One of the tools mentioned prior is to make sure you have a soft cloth or padded tray to place your coins on when looking at them. But it's good to have too just in case you do drop them because then at least they are on a soft surface.

I think it's important to mention cleaning of the coins – and the reason you shouldn't do that. While it may be tempting, it's essential to refrain from cleaning coins as cleaning can remove natural toning or patina that contributes to their value. Polishing and/or cleaning coins can reduce their value. Older coins that show deep age coloration are more desirable than coins whose surfaces have been stripped away by improper polishing or cleaning. However, if you do polish a coin to remove dirt, use mild soap and water. Once you've washed the coin, pat it dry with a soft towel. Brushing or rubbing can scratch a coin's delicate surface.

Storing Your Collection

Once you are working on a collection of coins, no matter the type of coins, it's a good idea to buy a few coin holders, tubes, or other types of containers to keep them looking their best. There are many different types of folders,

holders, albums, tubes, and so forth to hold your coins. If at all possible, purchase coin sets and coins in their original cases and capsules. The Mint provides coin sets in protective plastic cases called lenses or in folders. Individual coins are packaged in capsules fitted into folders or boxes. Professional coin grading services use sealed slabs to protect graded coins. When providing your own storage holders, always use acid-free cardboard and plastic holders free from polyvinyl chloride (PVC). Acid and PVC can ruin a coin's surface. Many times, your local coin shop and coin shows will have an assortment to choose from. It's a good idea to browse these to get an idea of what you like before you buy online or elsewhere.

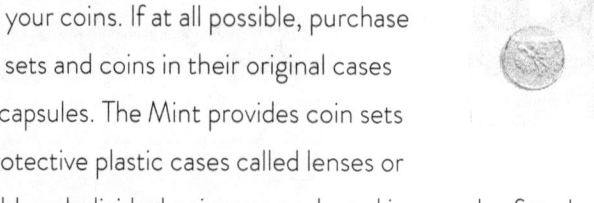
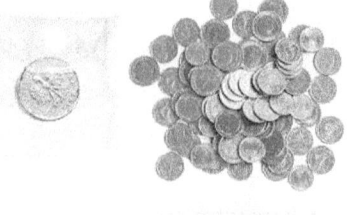

Along with obtaining some protective holders, you can choose the organization system that you prefer. For example, I buy plastic coin tubes to hold my 40% silver dimes, but I put my uncirculated W Mint quarters that I have found

by coin roll hunting in flip cardboards w/ clear faces. In these two examples, I am stacking my silver dimes and have 20 in a tube. At a glance, I can look at my tubes and know how many silver dimes are in my collection. However, I sell my W Mint quarters, sometimes individually and sometimes in bulk. Putting them in the cardboard flips protects them and makes them convenient to show, sell,

and ship. Again, everyone is unique with their own preferences. I may be a bit unusual in that I like to touch my coins and hold them often so I refrain from putting them into more permanent holders; however, my dad prefers graded coins in individual slabs – those you can't touch.

These coin holders come in various sizes and styles to accommodate different coin types, sizes, and collector preferences. Choosing the right holder depends on factors such as coin type, storage space, display preferences, and budget. This chart provides an overview of different types of coin holders and their features, helping collectors choose the best option for specific needs and preferences.

Coin Holder Type	What to Look For
Coin Flips	Small, transparent holders made of soft, pliable plastic. Coins are placed between two layers of plastic and sealed along the edges.
2x2 Cardboard Holders	Square cardboard holders with a clear window for viewing the coin. They are typically stapled shut to secure the coin in place.
Coin Tubes	Cylindrical containers made of durable plastic designed to hold and protect a large number of coins of the same denomination.
Coin Albums	Bound albums with clear plastic sheets or cardboard pages with pockets to hold individual coins. They often come with labeled slots for different coin types and years.
Air-Tite Holders	Hard plastic capsules that snap shut to encase individual coins securely, protecting them from dust, moisture, and scratches.
Coin Holders with Inserts	Plastic holders with removable inserts that allow for the display of coins along with informational lables or descriptions.
Coin Display Cases	Transparent acrylic cases with individual compartments or slots for displaying and protecting coins, often used for showcasing special or valuable pieces.

Coin Folders	Foldable cardboard folders with labeled slots for specific coin types and years, ideal for organizing and displaying complete sets.
Coin Storage Boxes	Sturdy cardboard or wooden boxes with compartments or trays to hold multiple coin holders or albums, providing additional protection and organization.
Coin Capsules	Hard, clear plastic capsules designed to fit individual coins snugly, providing a protective barrier against handling and enviornmental damage.

Documentation and Safety

Building up a coin collection can become a very important part of your life as well as being valuable. I believe keeping thorough documentation of your coin collection is beneficial for several reasons. Firstly, it helps you keep track of the coins you own, including their types, dates, mint marks, and any notable features or variations. This documentation serves as a valuable reference when assessing the value or authenticity of your coins, especially if you decide to sell or trade them in the future. Additionally, detailed documentation can be crucial for insurance purposes, providing evidence of the coins' existence and value in case of loss, theft, or damage. By maintaining accurate records, you can ensure that your collection is adequately protected and accounted for. Another reason would be for legacy reasons and helping family members who may inherit them.

Don't overlook safety as another critical aspect of coin collecting. When storing your coins, it's really important to choose a secure location that offers protection from theft, fire, and environmental factors like humidity and temperature fluctuations. I think investing in a fireproof safe is a real good idea to have at home or utilize a safety deposit box at a bank to safeguard your collection. Actually, do both!

Furthermore, be cautious when sharing information about your collection, especially online like in YouTube videos, Instagram, or any other social media outlet. The same goes with talking with others outside the home to avoid becoming a target for theft. In other words, don't advertise!

Transporting coins is also an issue we don't want to overlook. One day you may be interested in setting up at coin shows or needing to move your coins from one location to another location. If so, use protective cases or holders to prevent damage, and avoid displaying them in public unless necessary. This advice is also true when coin roll hunting and transporting coins in and out of banks. In fact, collectors may use a solid, heavy-duty carrier on wheels when going to the bank; however, just the fact of being at a bank, onlookers can probably make the assumption that a collector is carrying large amounts of coins. Because of this, the security guards can walk anyone carrying bank boxes to and from the car as an added safety precaution. With so much love and passion we are putting into coins, it only makes sense that we prioritize both documentation and safety measures.

CHAPTER ELEVEN

UNDERSTANDING COIN GRADING SCALES

Coin Grading

Coin grading is a crucial aspect of numismatics, helping collectors and investors assess the quality and value of their coins. The Sheldon coin grading scale, named after its creator Dr. William Sheldon, is widely used in the industry, although today it has been modified from its original version. This scale assigns a numerical grade ranging from 1 to 70 to each coin, along with a corresponding descriptive adjective such as "poor," "good," "very fine," or "mint state."

Several factors are taken into consideration when grading a coin, including the quality of its production, the amount of wear it has sustained over time, and its overall luster or brilliance. Coins in mint condition, with no signs of wear and a high degree of original luster, typically receive the highest grades, such as MS-70 (Mint State 70), indicating perfection.

Professional coin grading services play a significant role in the market, providing impartial assessments of coin quality and authenticity. However, it's important to recognize that coin grading is subjective to some extent, and different graders may assign slightly different grades to the same coin.

There are professional coin grading services, but as a collector, it's important to understand coin grading to know the value of a coin and to be familiar with the grading standards. Using resources such as the Official ANA Grading Standards for United States Coins, which began publishing their grading standards in 1977, collectors can gain valuable insights into the condition and rarity of their coins, as well as verify grades assigned by others.

Official ANA (American Numismatic Association) Grading Standards for United States Coins

The following comprehensive chart represents the Official ANA (American Numismatic Association) Grading Standards for United States Coins. These grades represent the condition and quality of a coin, ranging from Poor (1) to highest grade of perfection (MS-70). Alongside the grade is a description of the quality or "look" of the coin.

Coins Grading Scales and Descriptions Chart

Grade	Description	Contact Marks	Hairlines	Luster	Eye Appeal
MS-70	Perfect coin with sharp strike and original luster	None visible under magnification	None visible under magnification	Very attractive, fully original	Outstanding
MS-69	Attractive sharp strike, full original luster	1 or 2 minuscule, none in prime focal areas	None visible	Very attractive, fully original	Exceptional
MS-68	Attractive sharp strike, full original luster	3 or 4 minuscule, none in prime focal areas	None visible	Very attractive, fully original	Exceptional
MS-67	Original luster, normal strike	3 or 4 minuscule, 1 or 2 may be in prime focal areas	None visible without magnification	Very attractive, nearly fully original	Exceptional
MS-66	Above average quality of surface and mint luster	Several small, a few may be in prime focal areas	None visible without magnification	Very attractive, fully original	Above average
MS-65	High quality of luster and strike	Light and scattered without major distracting marks in prime focal areas	May have a few scattered	Very attractive, fully original	Very pleasing

Grade	Luster/Strike	Marks	Hairlines	Eye Appeal	Overall
MS-64	At least average luster and strike	May have light scattered marks; a few may be in prime focal areas	May have a few scattered or a small patch	Average	Quite attractive
MS-63	Mint luster may be slightly impaired	May have distracting marks in prime focal areas	May have a few scattered or a small patch	Maybe slightly impaired	Rather attractive
MS-62	Impaired or dull luster may be evident	May have distracting marks in prime focal areas/ or secondary areas	May have a few scattered or a noticeable patch	Maybe somewhat impaired	Generally acceptable
MS-61	Mint luster may be diminished or noticeably impaired	May have a few heavy (or numerous light) marks in prime focal and/ or secondary areas	May have noticeable patch or continuous hairlining over surfaces	Maybe impaired	Unattractive
MS-60	Unattractive, dull, or washed-out mint luster	May have heavy marks in all areas	May have noticeable patch or continuous hairlining overall	Often impaired	Poor
AU-58	Barest trace of wear, nearly full luster	No major detracting marks present	N/A	Attractive, nearly full	Often with appearance of higher grade
AU-55	Small patches of wear, above average surface	Very few contact marks or blemishes	N/A	Above average	Above average

Grade	Wear	Rim		Luster	Overall
AU-53	Noticeable spots of wear, diminished luster	Very few contact marks or blemishes	N/A	Diminished	Generally good
AU-50	Traces of wear, some original luster present	May have a few noticeable contact marks or flaws	N/A	Some original luster	Generally acceptable
EF-45	Light overall wear, sharp design details	All design details are very sharp	N/A	Usually seen only in protected areas	Very sharp
EF-40	Slight wear, excellent sharpness	All design elements show clearly	N/A	Traces may still show	All elements clear
VF-35	Light overall wear, minor blemishes	May have one or two small rim nicks	N/A	All details clear	Light overall wear
VF-30	Light wear, design details softening	Design details begin to soften	N/A	Design details begin to soften	Design details bold
VF-25	Signs of wear, softening design elements	All design details show clearly	N/A	Design elements softening	Design features clear
VF-20	Noticeable wear, minor details flattening	Minor details are beginning to flatten	N/A	Some minor details visible	Surfaces attractive
F-15	Moderate even wear, bold design	All design is bold and clear	N/A	Traces of flattening	Bold and clear
F-12	Moderate to considerable wear, bold design	All design is bold	N/A	May only show parts of letters	Bold design
VG-10	Even wear, readable features	Parts of the rim may be flat	N/A	Some letters readable	Major design visible

VG-8	Well worn, faintness in areas	Major design elements are visible	N/A	Outline form, without center detail	Mostly worn away
G-6	Heavily worn, attractive surfaces	May have a few rim nicks	N/A	Rims weak but complete	Clean and attractive
G-4	Heavily worn, faintness in areas	Major design elements are visible	N/A	Outline form, without center detail	May be incomplete
AG-3	Very heavily worn, barely readable	Portions worn smooth	N/A	Rims merge into lettering	Rims merge into lettering
Fair-2	Design worn smooth, legend merged into field	Worn completely smooth	N/A	Flat or missing rims	Numerous blemishes
Poor-1	Basic coin type identifiable, heavily worn	Worn smooth	N/A	Worn and disfigured	Date and mintmark readable

Abbreviations:

MS: Mint State

AU: About Uncirculated

EF: Extremely Fine

VF: Very Fine

F: Fine

VG: Very Good

G: Good

AG: About Good

Gaps in the Scale

Looking over the chart, you may have noticed that there are some numbers missing between 1 and 70. For instance, there are no numbers 5, 7, 11, 13-14, and 16-19. Then, starting at 20, it continues to go up in increments of 5. In the 50's range, it skips numbers 51-52, 54, 56-57, and 59. However, starting with 60, it goes all the way to 70 with no gaps to complete the scale. I wanted to point this out because many collectors wonder about this particular method. It has been stated that the numbers that are not designated on the scale avoids confusion and helps to maintain clarity in grading coins. The grading scale employs specific increments to categorize the condition of coins, and omitting certain numbers helps streamline the grading process and prevents unnecessary subdivisions within each grade category.

Grading Companies

Professional grading services also known as third-party grading (TPG), began in the 1980s to help coin collectors. Their main goals were to make grading more consistent, spot changes made to coins, and stop fake coins from circulating. These services charge different fees depending on what you want them to do with your coin. When a collector sends in coins to be graded, these services will evaluate coins based on various factors such as condition, rarity, and historical significance, assigning them a grade that reflects their overall quality. Additionally, they authenticate coins to ensure they are genuine and not counterfeit.

One of the key features of professional grading services is the encapsulation or "slabbing" of coins. After assessment and grading, coins are encapsulated in a sealed, tamper-evident plastic holder along with a label that displays important information such as the coin's grade, certification number, and other relevant

details. This process helps to protect the coin from damage and tampering while providing a convenient and standardized way to store and display graded coins.

Overall, certification services have made a big difference. They've lowered the number of fake coins and coins that are graded too high. This helps collectors trust what they're buying. But, considering that grading coins is subjective in nature, the grade is not always the same between different services. Even the same grading company might give a different grade if the coin is sent in again. Factors such as the toning, luster, or how well it was made aren't always considered or evaluated exactly the same.

Because small differences in a coin's condition can make a big difference in its value, some collectors send their coins to be graded again and again, hoping for a better grade but that comes at a cost. Collectors have to weigh if they should spend their money on buying new coins or spend money on grading.

Some of the most well-known professional grading services include:

Numismatic Guaranty Corporation (NGC): NGC is one of the leading coin grading services globally, known for its rigorous standards and expertise in grading both modern and vintage coins.

Professional Coin Grading Service (PCGS): PCGS is another prominent grading service trusted by collectors and dealers worldwide. It employs a team of highly experienced graders who meticulously evaluate coins using advanced technology and industry-leading standards.

Independent Coin Graders (ICG): ICG offers professional coin grading services with a focus on accuracy and consistency. It provides grading and authentication services for a wide range of coins, catering to both beginners and seasoned collectors.

American Numismatic Association Certification Service (ANACS): ANACS is operated by the American Numismatic Association and offers grading and authentication services for coins, medals, and tokens. It is one of the oldest grading services in the United States, with a rich history dating back to 1972.

Certified Acceptance Corporation (CAC): This third-party grading company was started by founder, John Albanese, who coincidently also started NGC and PCGS. Not only does this company do a grading service, but it also actually evaluates coins by other grading companies. Those coins that are deemed as high-end for their grades and appropriately graded by the other companies receive a green sticker, affectionately known as the "green bean" sticker. CAC-stickered coins are considered as the highest standard attainable for certified coins.

These professional grading services adhere to strict guidelines and standards established by industry organizations to ensure integrity and reliability in the coin grading process. Collectors often rely on certified and slabbed coins from these services to build their collections with confidence, knowing that their coins have been professionally evaluated and authenticated.

> *My Tip:* One useful factor that helps you keep track with your collection is that when you purchase a graded coin slab with one of the grading services stickers, such as PCGS, you can simply use your phone to go online to their site (after you've created an account) and take a picture of your coin's barcode and register it with your name as the owner. This helps you keep track of your coins and logs you as the owner!

This example is from a PCGS coin graded slab. This gives you an idea of how to read the labels from the grading companies.

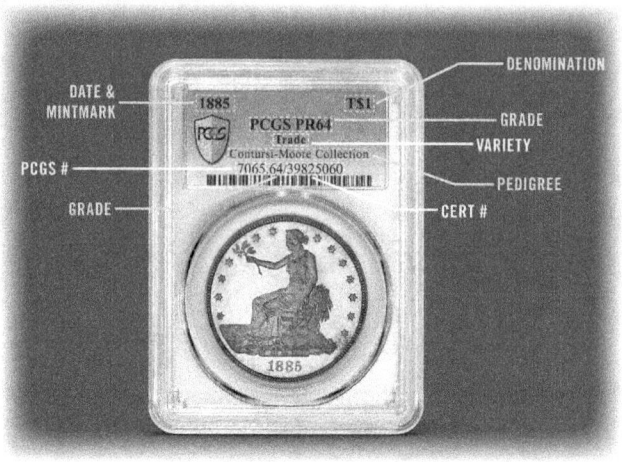

CHAPTER TWELVE

ERROR COINS

When we think of the word "error", we normally associate the term with a mistake or something of a negative factor, right? But, in numismatics, errors can be a positive! Some coin errors are valuable to collectors because they represent unique and often unexpected variations from the standard minting process. These deviations can range from minor imperfections to dramatic anomalies, making error coins as prized possessions in numismatics. For example, a coin with a double strike, where the design is partially repeated, or a misaligned die error, where the design is off-center, can fetch significant premiums due to their rarity and novelty. Additionally, error coins offer insights into the minting process and can shed light on the challenges faced by mint workers. Collectors value these coins not only for their monetary worth but also for their historical and educational significance in the realm of coin collecting.

One of the most famous examples of a coin error is the 1955 Lincoln cent, which was struck with a doubled die error. In this case, the obverse die was incorrectly hubbed with a slight rotation, causing parts of the design to appear doubled. As a result, the date and the words "LIBERTY" and "IN GOD WE TRUST" on the coin exhibit a noticeable doubling effect, as well as in Lincoln's profile. The doubling gives the appearance of a shadow or outline next to the original design elements, creating a striking visual effect. This error was not caught during the night shift at the Philadelphia mint, and a small number of these doubled die coins entered circulation (20,000-24,000). Today, the 1955 doubled die Lincoln cent is highly sought after by collectors with only a very few existing in mint state and can command significant premiums depending on its condition and rarity.

Error Coins Classification System

The classification system for coin errors evolved over time as numismatists and collectors encountered various irregularities in coins. Initially, errors were identified informally by collectors who noticed unusual features or abnormalities in coins. However, Alan Herbert, a coin collector who began collecting coins in his 30s, became a pioneer in the field of error and variety coinage.

Mr. Herbert played a significant role in creating a classification system for coin errors through his work as a numismatic researcher and writer. He published several works including The Official Price Guide to Mint Errors, laying the foundation for modern error coin collecting. Herbert introduced a systematic approach to categorizing and identifying coin errors, including die varieties, die clashes, and other striking anomalies. Alan Herbert is credited with creating the "P-D-S" system of classifying coin errors. The "P-D-S" system refers to Planchet, Die, and Strike errors. The following graphs in this section will give examples of each type.

While Herbert's classification system was influential in the numismatic community and has served as a valuable reference for collectors and researchers, today numismatists use a more comprehensive classification system that incorporates advancements in technology, research, and understanding of coin errors. Organizations like the ANA catalogs and categorizes different types of errors to help collectors understand and classify them more systematically.

Planchet Errors

Errors occur during the early stages of making coins when metal strips are turned into coin blanks, or planchets. These errors can cause the planchets to be misshapen, too large or small, or made from the wrong metal for the coin's denomination. Sometimes, the metals in a planchet are mixed incorrectly, leading to a

part of the coin's surface appearing to "peel" away, known as a lamination error. This can give older cents a unique wood-grain appearance. Planchet errors result in distinct and often rare coin variations due to their irregularities in shape, size, and composition.

Common types of planchet errors:

Type of Planchet Error	Description
Blank Planchet	Coin disks punched out from metal strips. Type-1 blanks lack rounded rims, while Type-2 blanks have uniform rounded rims added.
Clipped Planchet	Occurs when the metal strip is misfed through the blanking machine, resulting in straight or curved clips on the planchet's edges.
Improper Thickness	Planchets struck on blanks that are either too thin or too thick, leading to underweight or overweight coins.
Lamination Flaw	Defect caused by metal impurities or internal stresses, resulting in discoloration, uneven surfaces, peeling, and splitting of the planchet.
Split Planchet	Occurs when impurities become trapped under the planchet's surface, creating weaknesses or defects that may flake, peel, or split before or after striking.

Cladding Flaw	Irregularities in the layers of different merals known as clads, which can peel, fold, or separate, resulting in irregularities on the coin's surface.

Hub and Die Errors

Hub and dies are essential tools used by the U.S. Mint to create the intricate designs found on coins and medals. Rather than etching each design individually, the Mint employs a pressing method. A die is a stamp used to imprint the design onto the coins or medals. To produce the die itself, the Mint utilizes another stamp known as a hub, which transfers the design onto the die.

During the coin manufacturing process, hub and die errors can occur, resulting in abnormalities in the finished coins. A common error is when dies fracture, creating intricate cracks resembling lightning bolts on the coin's surface. Another type of error, called cuds, arises when sections of the die break near the coin's edges, causing a distorted, blob-like shape on the coin.

Additionally, dirt or grease may become trapped in the recesses of the die, leading to filled-in areas on the coin's design, which appear as if parts of the image are missing. These errors can affect the appearance and value of the coins produced. A great example of this error occurred in 1922, when only the Denver mint struck Lincoln cents. As a result of the mint attempting to speed up production, an excessive amount of grease was applied to the dies. So much grease in fact that the mintmark was obscured making it either nonexistent or weakened. These 1922 cents are very popular with collectors and obtaining one makes it a cherished addition to any collection.

Common types of hub and die errors:

Type of Hub and Die Error	Description
Fundamental Die-Setting Error	Die is not set as intended, resulting in errors like misquoted inscriptions or incorrect designs on the coins.
Missing Design Elements	Errors caused by missing mintmarks, dates, or other design elements due to issues in the die or during the striking process.
Doubled Die	Additional, misaligned impression from the hub results in doubling of design portions, or distorted images on the coins.
Die Defects	Includes cracks, breaks, and chips in the dies, leading to raised lines, missing portions, or distorted images on the coins.
Die Clash	Observe and reverse dies collide without a planchet between them, causing parts of one die's image to be impressed on the other.
MAD Clash	Misaligned dies strike each other while misaligned, causing errors in the coin's design and details.
Punching Errors	Historical errors caused by manual addition of design elements to dies using punches, resulting in doubled images or incorrect letters/ numbers on the coins.
Overdates and Overmintmarks	Result from intentional recycling of dies or addition of new mintmarks over existing ones, leading to coins with multiple dates or mintmarks.
Trails	Lines on coins caused by modern high-pressure "single pressing" process, resulting in visible lines on the coins known as trails.
Mule	Coins struck with dies never intended for use together, such as dies designed for different coin denominations or with missing date inscriptions.

| Misaligned Dies | Errors occur when dies are offset, titles, or rotated, resulting in coins with off-centered designs, missing elements, or rotated images. |

Strike Errors

Strike errors manifest during the coin production process when the planchet, or blank metal disc, is struck by the dies. These errors occur within the coin striking chamber and can stem from various factors. For instance, if a coin isn't centered correctly within the chamber, if it becomes lodged in the press and sustains repeated blows from the dies, or if foreign material becomes trapped between the planchet and a die during striking, it can lead to these irregularities in the final coins.

One notable example that could be considered a planchet error as well as a strike error is the 1943 Lincoln cent, which was supposed to be made of zinc-coated steel due to the shortage of copper during World War II. However, some copper planchets intended for 1942 cents remained in the coining presses and were struck with the new 1943 dies, creating a rare and valuable error known as the "1943 bronze cent."

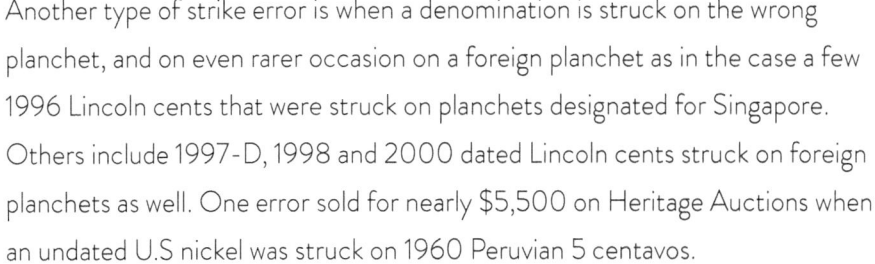

Another type of strike error is when a denomination is struck on the wrong planchet, and on even rarer occasion on a foreign planchet as in the case a few 1996 Lincoln cents that were struck on planchets designated for Singapore. Others include 1997-D, 1998 and 2000 dated Lincoln cents struck on foreign planchets as well. One error sold for nearly $5,500 on Heritage Auctions when an undated U.S nickel was struck on 1960 Peruvian 5 centavos.

Common types of strike errors:

Type of Strike Error	Description
Broadstrike	Collar die malfunction leads to coins with plain edges.
Strike Through	Another object comes between blank planchet and die, leaving an impression on the coin's surface.
Uni-face Coin	Two planchets stacked during striking result in coins with images on only one side.
Die Cap	Struck coin remains on die, leaving impression on subsequent coins.
Brockage	Mirror image of a coin struck on a black planchet due to ejection failure.
Edge Strike	Standing or chain edge strikes due to blank bouncing or expanding between dies.
Multiple Strike	Coin receives additional strikes, resulting in additional images.
Off-center Strike	Coins struck-off center, leading to non-circular shapes.
Double Denomination	Coins struck twice between different denomination dies, resulting in coins with two denominations.
Struck on Wrong Planchet	Planchets for one denomination fed into press with dies of another denomination, resulting in incorrect designed or compositions.
Edge and Rim Errors	Result from collars being out of position or deteriorated, leading to issues like wire rims or partial collars.
Mated Pair or Set	Collection of coins struck together, related due to resulting errors.

Coin errors, whether stemming from planchet, hub and die, or striking mishaps, add an intriguing dimension to the world of coin collecting. These anomalies, often resulting from unforeseen circumstances or mistakes in the production process, have captivated collectors for centuries as each error tells a unique story of the minting process. Whether it's a rare double strike, a misaligned planchet, or a cracked die, these errors remind us of the human element behind the creation of every coin, making them valued treasures for enthusiasts worldwide.

CHAPTER THIRTEEN

COINS AND INFLATION: A CLOSER LOOK

Ever wondered how the value of your coins reflects the ebb and flow of the economy? There is a dynamic connection, kind of like a two-step dance, between economics and numismatics and even more specifically, coins and inflation. Many investors and coin collectors understand that overall, inflation has a profound impact of on coinage, including its influence on coin values. As mentioned earlier in the book, one reason that people will collect coins is to protect against inflation. Here, we'll examine a little bit closer look on why that is the case.

Understanding Inflation

First, we must understand how inflation is defined. Simply put, inflation is like a silent force that affects how much our money can buy over time. Have you noticed that the price of your favorite candy keeps going up every year? – that's inflation! When prices rise, the purchasing power of your money decreases, meaning you can buy less with the same amount of cash.

But why does inflation happen? Well, it's influenced by different things like how much people want to buy (demand), how much of something is available (supply), and even decisions made by the government. When you notice prices creeping up, you'll know that inflation is at work, and that is quietly shaping the value of your coins and of course, your purchasing power.

Impact of Inflation on Coins

Not only is inflation visible at the grocery stores, but I have noticed the impact at the coin shows too. Since inflation means that the value of money goes down over time, consequently, collectors may need to spend more money to acquire the same coins they could have purchased for less in the past.

Production Costs

The "flip side" (pun intended) is that it's not just about what you can buy – inflation also affects how much it costs to make coins, including the various aspects of coin production and distribution. For example, Mints incur higher expenses for acquiring raw materials, such as metals used in coin production, as well as for labor and operational costs. These increased production costs are often passed on to collectors who have to pay more for newly minted coins.

Pricing Dynamics

Inflation also extends beyond the primary market for newly minted coins to the secondary market for collectible coins influencing the pricing dynamics within the collector market itself. As the general price level rises, collectors may adjust their buying and selling behaviors in response to changes in affordability and perceived value. Additionally, inflation can contribute to speculative activity within the collector market. Prices for rare and valuable coins may experience upward pressure as collectors and investors allocate more funds towards tangible assets as a hedge against inflation. Conversely, coins with lower intrinsic value or less numismatic appeal may see relatively slower price growth or even depreciation in real terms.

Coping with Inflation: Coin Collecting Strategies

Coping with any economic challenge like inflation really requires everyone to adjust and adopt strategies to help themselves, and coin collectors do the same. Numismatists aim to preserve the value of their collections while still trying to add to their collections by using smart approaches amidst monetary fluctuations.

Diversifying

One effective method is diversification, which involves acquiring coins across different categories, denominations, and time periods. By spreading out investments across a diverse range of coins, collectors can lessen the risks associated with inflation affecting specific segments of the market.

For instance, consider a collector who primarily focuses on modern U.S. coins and has built up an extensive collection of Lincoln cents, Jefferson nickels, and Roosevelt dimes from the 20th and 21st centuries. As inflation begins to rise, the collector becomes concerned about the potential impact on the value of their collection. To mitigate this risk, he decides to diversify his coin holdings by adding coins from different categories, denominations, and time periods, including ancient Roman coins, silver dollars from the 19th century, and commemorative coins from various countries. By spreading investments across a broader range of coins, each with its own unique historical significance and market dynamics, the collector lessens the risks associated with inflation affecting specific segments of the coin market.

Shifting to a Rare/Historical Coin Focus

Focusing on rare and historically significant coins is another valuable strategy for navigating inflationary pressures. Coins with unique historical backgrounds, limited

mintages, or iconic designs often retain their value or appreciate over time, regardless of fluctuations in the broader economy. For example, rare coins like the 1909-S VDB Lincoln Cent or the 1916-D Mercury Dime have consistently commanded high prices among collectors due to their scarcity and historical importance. As individuals seek to hedge against the eroding value of currency, they may increase their investing in tangible assets like rare coins.

Staying Informed on Up-to-Date Trends
Staying informed about economic trends and developments is crucial for coin collectors seeking to anticipate potential shifts in the coin market and adjust their strategies accordingly. If collectors regularly follow financial news and economic reports, they have a tendency to notice a significant uptick in inflation rates and anticipate that this could impact the value of their coin collection. To stay informed, they regularly check reputable sources such as financial news websites, government publications, and numismatic forums for updates on inflation rates, interest rate changes, and currency fluctuations. Armed with this knowledge, collectors may decide to adjust their collecting strategy by focusing more on acquiring gold and silver coins, which are traditionally seen as hedges against inflation. By staying vigilant and adapting to economic trends, collectors can better navigate the challenges posed by inflationary conditions and safeguard the value of their coin collection.

Predicting Future by Studying the Past
This strategy goes hand-in-hand with the previous strategy. Although this may seem like an overly used statement, it remains verifiable that understanding historical trends can help collectors anticipate future economic conditions and their impact on coin values. By analyzing past economic cycles, inflation rates, and market behaviors, collectors can then gain valuable insights into potential future developments. For example, studying historical data on coin prices during periods of high inflation can provide clues about which types of coins tend to retain their value or appreciate in such environments. Additionally, examining

past instances of economic downturns or currency crises can help collectors prepare for similar scenarios in the future.

Explore Alternative Ways to Invest

Besides the other strategies, collectors can additionally explore alternative avenues for preserving the value of their coin collections. One option a collector may consider is investing in precious metals like gold and silver bullion that has historically served to circumvent inflation and currency devaluation, offering a tangible store of wealth in times of economic uncertainty. To stay informed about precious metal prices and trends, the collector will regularly check financial news websites, precious metal market reports, and online bullion dealers' websites.

Another avenue a collector may explore is investing in numismatic funds, which are managed by experienced numismatists, provide investors with exposure to diversified portfolios of rare coins, offering potential returns while mitigating individual coin risks. To research numismatic funds, the collector will consult investment websites, speak with financial advisors, and attend numismatic conferences or seminars.

Through a careful examination of history, by diversifying holdings, focusing on rare coins, staying informed about current economic trends, and exploring alternative investment options, collectors can navigate the range of monetary fluctuation and continue to enjoy the enduring appeal of numismatics. When used consistently, these methods not only help during inflation, but should be used even in "good times" to help negate the effect when economic uncertainty does occur. Numismatists can then make informed and confident decisions about buying, selling, and managing their coin collections.

CHAPTER FOURTEEN

NAVIGATING MISNOMERS IN THE COIN MARKET

Identifying Coins and Misconceptions

In the world of coin collecting, it's not uncommon to encounter coins that may appear valuable at first glance but, upon closer inspection, turn out to be less significant. In this section, we'll explore some common factors that contribute to a coin's perceived value and how collectors can differentiate between coins with genuine worth and those with only superficial appeal.

Several factors can contribute to the perceived value of a coin, including its age, condition, rarity, and historical significance. However, collectors should be wary of placing too much emphasis on these factors alone, as they may not always accurately reflect a coin's true worth. For example, while an old coin may seem valuable due to its age, its actual rarity and demand among collectors are what ultimately determine its market value.

One common misconception among novice collectors is the belief that all old coins are inherently valuable. While age can certainly add to a coin's appeal, it does not guarantee its worth. Similarly, coins in pristine condition may appear valuable, but factors such as mintage numbers and collector demand play a more significant role in determining their value.

The key to avoiding the pitfalls of investing in seemingly valuable but ultimately worthless coins is education. Collectors should take the time to research and familiarize themselves with the factors that contribute to a coin's true value. This includes studying mintage figures, historical context, and current market trends. By becoming knowledgeable about the nuances of coin collecting, collectors can make more informed decisions and avoid falling victim to scams or overpaying for coins with little actual worth.

When in doubt, it's always a good idea to seek advice from experienced collectors or numismatic professionals. These individuals can offer valuable insights and help assess the true value of a coin based on their expertise and knowledge of the market. Additionally, joining collector forums or attending coin shows can provide opportunities to learn from others and gain valuable insights into the world of coin collecting.

While the allure of owning rare or valuable coins is undeniable, collectors must exercise caution and diligence when evaluating potential acquisitions. By understanding the factors that contribute to a coin's true value and seeking expert guidance when needed, collectors can build collections that are both enjoyable and financially rewarding. Remember, appearances can be deceiving, so always look beyond the surface when assessing a coin's worth.

Types of Coins with Commonly Mistaken Values

Common Date Coins in Average Condition

Some coins, particularly those from widely circulated series like modern Lincoln cents or Jefferson nickels, may appear valuable due to their age but are actually quite common and readily available. For example, an old 1950s Lincoln cent in average circulated condition has high mintage numbers giving it little intrinsic value beyond its face value.

Replica or Replica-like Coins

Occasionally, collectors may encounter coins that resemble valuable or rare issues but are actually modern reproductions or replicas. These coins may be intentionally misleading or marketed as novelty items. For instance, replica gold coins bearing famous designs like the Saint-Gaudens double eagle or the Liberty Head nickel may appear valuable to inexperienced collectors but lack the authenticity and precious metal content of genuine coins.

Coins with Excessive Wear or Damage

Coins that exhibit significant wear, damage, or alterations may appear valuable at first glance due to their age or design but are actually worth little to collectors. For example, a heavily worn Morgan silver dollar with a smooth, flat surface may seem valuable because it is old and has silver content, but its numismatic value is greatly diminished by its condition.

Coins with Counterfeit or Altered Features

Unfortunately, counterfeit coins are a prevalent issue in the numismatic world, and inexperienced and seasoned collectors may inadvertently acquire counterfeit or altered coins that appear genuine. For instance, a counterfeit Gold or Silver Eagle may have convincing details but lacks the authenticity of a genuine issue, making it essentially worthless to collectors.

Coins with Common Errors

While some error coins can be highly valuable, others are relatively common and have little numismatic significance. For example, a Lincoln cent with a minor misalignment in the mintmark or a slightly off-center strike may seem interesting but is unlikely to command a significant premium in the collector market.

Coins That Appear Valuable But Aren't

Some coins when found give the illusion that they must be valuable because they are uncommon on a daily basis. Despite their appearance or commemorative nature, not all coins hold significant value in the numismatic world. Here are some typical coins that may fool a rookie coin collector.

Coin	Description
Lincoln Wheat Pennies	While order wheat pennies may seem valuable, they typically trade for near face value, with the exception of a few key ones like the 1943-D Lincoln bronze wheat penny.
Pre-1965 Nickels	Unlike dimes, quarters, and half dollars from the same period, pre-1965 nickels do not contain silver and are typically only worth face value.
Bicentennial Quarters	Despite being produced as a special edition series, most bicentennial quarters from 1975-1976 are only worth face value, with rare exceptions like the 1976-S bicentennial silver quarter.
Kennedy Half Dollars	While low mintages might suggest value, Kennedy half dollars are typically only worth face value, unless minted from 1964-1970 which contain silver making their value worth more.
Eisenhower Silver Dollars	Although occasionally found in circulation, Eisenhower silver dollars are often considered too large and inconvenient by collectors, resulting in relatively low value.
Susan B. Anthony Dollars	Despite being the first U.S. coins to depict a non-fictional woman, most Susan B. Anthony dollars are only worth face value due to high supply and low demand.
Sacagawea & Presidential Dollars	Although some Sacagawea and Presidential dollars have gold-like appearances, they are made of manganese brass and are typically only worth face value.

State Quarters	While the State Quarters program generated widespread interest, most state quarters are only worth face value due to their high mintage numbers and availability.
Double Denomination	Coins struck twice between different denomination dies, resulting in coins with two denominations.
Struck on Wrong Planchet	Planchets for one denomination fed into press with dies of another denomination, resulting in incorrect designed or compositions.

Lincoln Wheat Pennies

It can be exciting to find a Lincoln Wheat Penny in your pocket change because you don't come across that many in everyday life. These coins were struck between 1909 and 1958, so even the most recent versions are more than 60 years old. If you come across a 1943-D Lincoln bronze wheat penny, you could find yourself a whole lot richer. But even though these coins have largely disappeared from circulation, they haven't appreciated much in value on the collectibles market. They often trade in bulk for less than 5 cents each.

Pre-1965 Nickels

Pre-1965 dimes, quarters and half dollars have melt value because of their silver content, but that's not the case with pre-1965 nickels. These are made of nickel and copper, which are not as highly valued as silver. The only exceptions are nickels made between 1941-1945, which carry a premium because they hold a small amount of silver. The others won't bring much beyond face value.

Bicentennial Quarters

The U.S. Mint produced bicentennial quarters between 1975 and 1976 as a special edition series commemorating the nation's 200th birthday. They were notable for being the first U.S. quarters in more than 50 years to feature a special reverse design. The most valuable of those coins — a 1976-S bicentennial silver quarter that came in with a very high grade — sold for

$19,200 at auction a few years ago. But, that's the exception. Although these coins had limited circulation, they are not prized by collectors. The vast majority are only worth face value.

Kennedy Half Dollars

You don't see a lot of half dollars in circulation, which should boost their value you might think. Kennedy half dollars were first produced in 1964 following the assassination of President John F. Kennedy, replacing the Benjamin Franklin fifty-cent piece. Mintages of the Kennedy half dollars are low compared to other coins — but not low enough to make them valuable. The main exceptions are those produced from 1964-1970, which contain some amount of silver.

Eisenhower Silver Dollars

Dollar coins are another variety that can be fun to run across because you don't see them that often — including the Eisenhower silver dollar. The problem is, collectors and dealers consider the Eisenhower coin too large and clunky. The coin is deemed more inconvenient than anything else. Because they are also in massive qualities, their value gets dampened even further. Proof and silver editions are worth a bit, however.

Susan B. Anthony Dollars

Susan B. Anthony dollars are prized by historians and others because they are the first U.S. coins to depict a non-fictional woman. These coins were minted from 1979 to 1981 and again in 1999 to honor the women's rights advocate, abolitionist and champion of fair labor laws.

Some of the Susan B. Anthony Dollars are worth up to $500, but the vast majority have not caught on with collectors. One problem is that their smaller size and metal content are too close to the size and content of a quarter. Few people used them unless they accidentally confused them with quarters. In

addition, the U.S. government set aside a stockpile of 500 million coins before any others were released, meaning supply is high while demand is low.

Sacagawea & Presidential Dollars

Sacagawea and Presidential dollars are modern coin series with gold-like appearances. However, despite their metallic appearance, they are made of manganese brass and are typically only worth face value. Introduced in 2000, the Sacagawea dollar features a portrait of the Shoshone guide Sacagawea on the obverse and a soaring eagle on the reverse. Presidential dollars, minted from 2007 to 2016, honor former U.S. presidents with their portraits on the obverse and a rendition of the Statue of Liberty on the reverse.

State Quarters

The State Quarters program, launched in 1999, commemorated each of the 50 states with unique reverse designs on the quarter dollar. While these quarters generated widespread interest and are often collected, the vast majority are only worth face value. Despite their appealing designs and the occasional error or variety, most state quarters do not hold significant value beyond their denomination due to their high mintage numbers and widespread availability.

Spotting Counterfeits

It is quite unfortunate that in the world of coin collecting, there's a risk of coming across fake coins made by counterfeiters. These fake coins can trick collectors and hurt the trust within the coin-collecting community. To avoid this, it's important to learn how to spot counterfeit coins and protect your collection. Here are some tips to help you stay safe.

Firstly, get to know the coins you collect really well. Look closely at real coins to understand their details, like their weight, size, and intricate design details. This way, you can easily notice if something doesn't look right on a coin. For

instance, if you collect Morgan silver dollars, examine the distinct features of their portraits and inscriptions.

When you're buying new coins, take the time to examine it carefully. Look for any signs that it might be fake, like weird marks or differences from real coins. Special tools, like magnifying glasses or scales, can help you with this.

Also, make sure to get them from trusted sellers. These could be reputable dealers, renowned auction houses, or reputable online platforms with a track record of selling authentic coins. Always ask for certificates of authenticity if needed to prove that the coins are real.

Be cautious if you find a deal that seems too good to be true. If someone is selling coins at really low prices, this may be a red flag for counterfeit coins. For instance, if you come across a rare gold coin being sold at a fraction of its market value, it's essential to investigate further and verify its authenticity before making a purchase.

Stay up to date with what's happening in the coin-collecting world. Joining forums or talking to other collectors can help you learn about new scams and ways to spot counterfeit coins. If you're ever unsure about a coin's authenticity, don't hesitate to ask for help from professionals. There are experts who can check if a coin is real or fake, giving you peace of mind about your collection.

CHAPTER FIFTEEN

BUYING AND SELLING COINS

Navigating the numismatic marketplace requires diligence, research, and patience. Further, the process of selling coins requires careful consideration of factors such as market demand, pricing strategies, and preferred selling methods. When buying and selling coins, collectors should remember to prioritize authenticity, value, and personal preferences when making purchasing decisions, and don't hesitate to seek advice from seasoned collectors and professionals in the field.

Where to Buy and Sell Coins

In the world of coin collecting, knowing where to buy and sell coins is essential for building a successful collection and making informed decisions. Here, we'll explore various avenues for buying and selling coins, ranging from traditional brick-and-mortar dealerships to online platforms and auctions.

Local Coin Shops

Local coin shops, also known as LCSs, are excellent places to start your numismatic adventure. These stores offer a wide selection of coins and provide the opportunity to establish relationships with knowledgeable dealers who can offer guidance and expertise. Visiting an LCS allows you to examine coins in person, ask questions, and potentially negotiate prices. I also think it is simply a good practice to

Witter Coin Shop, "America's Coin Shop" San Francisco, CA

buy from your local coin shop which helps support the local community.

These local coin shops not only serve as great places to buy coins but also offer opportunities to sell pieces from your collection. Establishing relationships with LCS dealers can be advantageous when it comes time to sell, as they may offer

to buy from you with fair prices based on their knowledge of the market and condition of your coins. Additionally, selling to an LCS allows for immediate payment and avoids the complexities of shipping and online transactions.

Online Marketplaces
With the everyday buying of products (even groceries!) on the internet, online marketplaces have become popular for buying and selling coins as well. Platforms like eBay, Heritage Auctions, and GreatCollections offer vast selections of coins from the U.S. and around the world. When buying online, it's important to research sellers' reputations, review return policies, and verify coin authenticity before making a purchase.

When listing coins for sale online, it's crucial to provide clear and accurate descriptions, including photographs that showcase the coin's condition and any notable features. Researching current market prices and setting competitive listing prices can help attract potential buyers and maximize selling opportunities.

Auction Houses
Auction houses host regular sales featuring rare and collectible coins. Participating in auctions can be an exciting way to acquire unique pieces for your collection. Major auction houses like Stack's
Bowers Galleries and Heritage Auctions conduct live and online auctions, allowing collectors to bid on coins from the comfort of their homes. Keep in mind that auction prices may include buyer's premiums, so factor these costs into your bidding strategy.

When considering using these auction houses to sell coins, understand that they usually offer consignment services. Although they get a percentage of the selling price, it does expose coins to a global audience of collectors and potentially achieve higher sale prices. Another advantage is that auction houses typically handle all aspects of the selling process, including cataloging, marketing, managing the auction, and facilitating payments.

Coin Shows

Probably my favorite way to buy and sell (and sometimes trade) coins is to attend coin shows. Dealers and collectors of every sort come together at these events offering a diverse array of coins, ranging from ancient to modern. Not only can you choose  to buy from a wide variety of coins, but it is also an opportunity to network with other enthusiasts. Coin shows often feature educational seminars, exhibits, and sometimes offer grading services, making them valuable learning experiences for collectors of all levels.

Participating in coin shows presents an opportunity to sell coins directly to collectors and dealers in a face-to-face setting. Setting up a table or booth at a coin show allows you to showcase your collection and engage with potential buyers. Be prepared to negotiate prices and provide documentation or certification for high-value coins to instill confidence in buyers. Coin shows also attract specialized buyers interested in specific coin types or themes so if you have a niche, it is a great place to set up.

Numismatic Forums and Communities

Online forums and social media groups dedicated to coin collecting provide platforms for enthusiasts to connect, share knowledge, and buy/sell/trade coins.

There are websites like CoinTalk which host discussions on various numismatic topics and offer classified sections where members can conduct transactions. Participating in these communities allows collectors to learn from others' experiences and stay informed about market trends.

When selling coins in any online community, transparency and honesty are paramount to building trust with buyers. Providing detailed descriptions, photographs, and pricing information can facilitate smooth transactions and positive interactions.

Specialty Dealers and Numismatic Associations
For collectors interested in specific coin types or themes, specialty dealers and numismatic associations offer specialized expertise and resources. Whether you're passionate about ancient coins or a particular series, seeking out dealers and organizations focused on your area of interest can enhance your collecting experience and help you find unique coins to purchase.

Some of these specialty dealers and associations may offer opportunities to consign or sell coins through their networks. Researching and contacting dealers or organizations relevant to your collection can lead to potential selling opportunities and access to niche markets. Selling through specialty channels may attract collectors with a keen interest in your coins' unique attributes or historical significance.

CHAPTER SIXTEEN

ETHICS IN NUMISMATICS

As we have gone deep into the multifaceted world of coin collecting, it's important to pause and reflect on the ethical considerations that underpin this amazing hobby. While the pursuit of rare and valuable coins often takes center stage, the principles of integrity, honesty, and respect for fellow collectors form the bedrock of our numismatic endeavors. Upholding ethical standards ensures fairness and trust within the hobby, ultimately contributing to its longevity and reputation. No buyer, no seller, no collector, no coin shop owner, no dealer, no company or anyone else should be associated with the business or hobby side of coins without permeating ethical standards.

Ethical Standards

In essence, ethical conduct in numismatics reflects a commitment to uphold certain held belief systems and actions within the community of coin collectors. Whether you own a coin shop or trade with some other collectors, there are certain principles that adhere to the Golden Rule – "Do unto others as you wish them do unto you." These standards help the entire community as a whole and enable us all to enjoy this hobby, passion, and lifestyle.

Authenticity and Disclosure

At the heart of ethical coin collecting is the commitment to authenticity and full disclosure. Sellers have a moral obligation to accurately represent the coins they offer for sale, including any defects, alterations, or restoration work. Providing clear and honest descriptions, accompanied by high-quality images, helps buyers make informed decisions and fosters trust between collectors and sellers.

Fair Pricing

Fair pricing is crucial to ethical coin transactions. Sellers should strive to set prices that reflect the true value of the coin based on its condition, rarity, and market demand. Manipulating prices or taking advantage of buyers' lack of knowledge damages the reputation of the seller and the hobby as a whole.

Respect for Fellow Collectors

Respecting fellow collectors involves treating them with courtesy, fairness, and honesty. This includes refraining from engaging in deceptive practices such as cherry-picking, where valuable coins are removed from a group lot before sale or misrepresenting the condition or rarity of coins to potential buyers. Building positive relationships with other collectors enriches the numismatic community and generates a spirit of camaraderie.

Due Diligence in Acquisition

Collectors have a responsibility to conduct due diligence when acquiring coins, especially high-value or rare pieces. This involves researching the provenance, authenticity, and market value of the coins before making a purchase. Consulting reputable experts, reference materials, and online resources can help collectors make informed decisions and avoid potential pitfalls.

Preservation and Conservation

Ethical collectors prioritize the preservation and conservation of coins for future generations. This includes handling coins with care to avoid damage, storing them in appropriate conditions to prevent deterioration, and respecting the historical and cultural significance of each piece. Overcleaning, altering, or tampering with coins diminishes their value and erases valuable historical context.

Contributing to the Hobby

Ethical collectors contribute to the growth and sustainability of the hobby by sharing knowledge, supporting educational initiatives, and participating in numismatic organizations and events. By cultivating an environment of inclusivity, learning, and mutual respect, collectors ensure that numismatics remains a vibrant and enriching pursuit for enthusiasts of all ages.

In essence, ethical conduct in numismatics reflects a commitment to integrity, transparency, and mutual respect among collectors, dealers, and stakeholders. By upholding these principles, individuals contribute to the preservation and enjoyment of coin collecting.

FINAL THOUGHTS

Starting as a young numismatist, I've been exploring the fascinating world of coin collecting and have had the privilege of meeting some of the best people, true icons in the industry. This is beyond just a hobby for me, it is a passion. And, it all started with a penny I found in some change! There are more stories of coins to uncover, and I personally can't wait for the next coin roll hunt.

I am always learning and am grateful for those that have and continue to help me along the way. It is my hope that I can teach and share my excitement for coin collection with others. I truly hope this book has inspired you. Whether it's the thrill of uncovering a rare coin, the camaraderie of fellow collectors, or the passing on of our passion to future generations, numismatics enhances our lives in ways we never could imagine.

I encourage you to continue your numismatic pathway with curiosity, enthusiasm, and an unwavering commitment to integrity. Let each coin you pick up and collect be a testament to the stories it holds, the history it represents, and the legacy it leaves behind.

Remember, the true value of a coin isn't measured in its monetary worth alone but in the knowledge, joy, and connections it brings to our lives. I hope your pockets are always full and your pursuit of coins be as rewarding as it is enriching.

Thank you for joining me on this remarkable journey. Here's to many more years of exploration, discovery, and delight in the captivating world of coin collecting.

Happy Collecting!

Mario Conway

If inclined, please stay tuned to my next finds:

Instagram

instagram.com/mariojconway

YouTube

youtube.com/@mariojconway

COIN TERMINOLOGY GLOSSARY

Alloy: A mixture of two or more metals used in the production of coins to achieve desired properties such as durability or color.

American Numismatic Association (ANA): nonprofit educational organization that educates people about coins and currency, and it provides resources for coin collectors and enthusiasts.

Annealing: Heating blanks (planchets) to a specific temperature and then cooled slowly to make them softer and more malleable for the coin striking process to reduce the risk of cracking or damaging the metal during coin production.

Assay: The process of testing and verifying the authenticity and purity of precious metals used in coin production, such as gold or silver.

Bag Mark: A scratch, dents, or abrasions found on the surface of coins from contact with other coins in a mint bag.

Bi-Metallic: Coins composed of two different metals or alloys bonded together.

Blank: A blank is a metal disc or planchet used in coin production before it is struck by coin dies to create a finished coin.

Bullion: Precious metals, typically platinum, gold or silver, in the form of bars, ingots, or coins, traded for their intrinsic value.

Bullion Coin: A coin made from precious metals, such as gold, silver, platinum, or palladium, and valued primarily based on its metal content rather than its rarity or numismatic value.

Business Strike: A coin intended for circulation, produced for general use rather than special editions or proofs, typically lacking the special finish or quality of proof coins

Bust: The portrait or image of a person's head, typically on the obverse (front) side of a coin.

Circulated: Coins that have been used in everyday transactions and show signs of wear from circulation.

Clad Coinage: Coins made by bonding layers of different metals together.

Coin: A piece of metal, usually round and stamped with a design, used as money or as a collectible item.

Collar: A metal ring or sleeve used in the coin production to hold the planchet in place during striking and to impart the reeded or lettered edge to the finished coin.

Commemorative: A coin issued to honor a specific person, event, or significant occasion.

Condition: The physical state or quality of a coin, including factors such as wear, damage, and overall appearance that is often graded on a scale from poor to mint condition.

Counterfeit: A fake or fraudulent coin made to resemble a genuine coin.

Currency: Coins or banknotes used as a medium of exchange in a particular country.

Denomination: The face value or monetary worth of a coin, typically indicated by its size and design.

Die: A steel rod with an engraved design (images, value, and mottoes) used to strike a blank piece of metal, typically paired with another die to imprint both sides to make a coin.

Designer: The individual responsible for creating the artistic design featured on a coin.

Edge: The outer border of a coin, considered the "third side" (not to be confused with "rim"), often containing reeding or lettering for identification.

Engraver: A skilled craftsman who carves or engraves the designs onto coin dies used for striking coins.

Error: A mistake or anomaly in the production of a coin, resulting in variations from the intended design or specifications.

Face Value: The nominal value of a coin, typically indicated by the denomination stamped on it.

Field: The flat or open area on a coin's surface not used for design or inscription, typically surrounding the raised design elements.

Grade: Rating which indicates how much a coin has worn from circulation, typically on a scale from poor to mint state.

Hairlines: Thin, shallow scratches or lines on the surface of a coin, often caused by improper handling or cleaning.

Incuse: A design element that is pressed into the surface of a coin, rather than raised above it.

Ingot: A bar or block of metal, typically gold or silver, used as a raw material for coin production or investment.

Inscription: Text or lettering stamped or engraved on a coin, typically indicating the issuing authority, denomination, or other relevant information.

Intrinsic Value (Bullion Value): The value of the metal content in a coin, based on its weight and purity.

Key Date: A coin that is rare or scarce within a particular series or set, often sought after by collectors.

Legal Tender: Coins or banknotes that are recognized by law as acceptable payment for debts or purchases.

Legend: Text or lettering on a coin, typically around the rim, conveying important information such as the country of issue, denomination, or date.

Medal: A metallic object similar to a coin but not intended for circulation, often awarded as a prize or commemorative item.

Medium of Exchange: Anything that is widely accepted as payment for goods and services, including coins, banknotes, and other forms of currency.

Mint: A place where coins are manufactured under government authority, including processes such as blanking, striking, and finishing.

Mint Luster: The shine or reflective quality of a coin's surface, typically resulting from its condition and preservation.

Mint Mark: A small letter stamped onto a coin, indicating the mint where it was produced.

Mint Set: A collection of coins produced by a particular mint for collectors, typically including coins of various denominations and conditions.

Mint State: The condition of a coin that has never been in circulation, retaining its original luster and surface quality; uncirculated.

Mintage: The total number of coins produced by a mint for a specific issue or series.

Motto: A phrase or slogan often found on coins, representing an ideology, national identity, or cultural sentiment such as, "E Pluribus Unum" inscribed on U.S. circulating coins which is Latin for "out of many, one."

Mylar®: A type of polyester film used in coin holders and protective sleeves to prevent damage and preserve coins.

Numismatics: The study or collecting of coins and things that are used as money, including their history, production, and valuation.

Obsolete: No longer in use or circulation, referring to coins that are no longer legal tender.

Obverse: The front (or "heads") side of a coin, usually featuring a portrait, emblem, or other design.

Off-Center: A coin struck with the design improperly aligned or positioned on the planchet.

Overstrike: A new coin produced by striking an older coin, typically resulting in a partial or double impression.

Patina: A thin layer of oxidation or discoloration that forms on the surface of a coin over time, often valued by collectors for its aesthetic appeal.

Pattern: A trial or experimental coin produced to test new designs, metals, or production techniques.

Planchet: The blank metal disk or piece prepared for striking into a coin.

Proof: A specially minted coin using highly polished dies and planchets, often struck more than once to accent the design and typically with mirror-like surfaces and sharp details, produced for collectors.

Proof Set: A collection of coins of each denomination made in a year produced using a special minting process to achieve a high level of detail and finish, often intended for collectors.

Rarity: The relative scarcity or uncommonness of a particular coin, often influencing its value.

Relief: The raised portion of a coin's design, contrasting with the recessed or incuse areas.

Restrike: A coin produced using original dies but struck at a later date than the original issue.

Reverse: The back (or "tails") side of a coin, usually featuring a different design than the obverse.

Riddler: A machine used to screen and sort out blanks or planchets for quality control in the coin production process.

Rim: The raised edge or border on both sides of a coin, designed to protect the coin's design and prevent wear.

Roll: A quantity of coins packaged together, typically by banks, dealers, or mints, often used for storage or transportation.

Series: A collection of coins that includes all date and mint mark variations for a specific design and denomination.

Slab: A protective coin holder or encapsulation method used to preserve and display coins, often made of plastic or acrylic.

Strike: The process of imprinting a design onto a planchet using a die or series of dies. The strength of the imprint – full, average, or weak – affects the value of rare coins.

Toning: The natural discoloration or patina that develops on the surface of a coin over time due to exposure to air, moisture, or other environmental factors.

Type Set: A collection of coins based on denomination, containing examples of each major coin type or design.

Uncirculated: Coins that have never been used in circulation and retain their original mint luster and condition.

Upsetting Mill: A machine used in the coin production process to raise the rim on both sides of a blank or planchet.

Variety: A subtype or minor difference within a particular coin issue, such as variations in design, mint mark placement, or errors.

Wear: The erosion or abrasion that occurs on a coin's surface over time, caused by handling, circulation, or environmental factors.

Year Set: A collection of coins produced by a mint in a specific year, typically including all denominations and varieties issued during that time.

www.ingramcontent.com/pod-product-compliance
Lightning Source LLC
Chambersburg PA
CBHW052300220526
45471CB00001B/421